**THE NANNY**, *53" x 32", #3-cut wool on rug warp. Designed and hooked by Elizabeth Black, Bentonville, Virginia, 1995.*

*To Gilbert, my late husband, whose support and*

*encouragement remain a constant force in my work,*

*and to Lisa, my daughter,*

*who is responsible for putting me on this path.*

# CONTENTS

*Rug Hooking Presents*

## HOOKED ON THE
# WILD SIDE

EDITION VIII of *RUG HOOKING*
MAGAZINE'S FRAMEWORK SERIES

*by Elizabeth Black*

**Editor**
*Virginia P. Stimmel*

**Book Designer**
*CW Design Solutions, Inc.*

**Assistant Editor**
*Lisa McMullen*

**Photography**
*Elizabeth Black*
*Impact Xpozures*

**Chairman**
*M. David Detweiler*

**Publisher**
*J. Richard Noel*

*Presented by*

# RUG HOOKING

1300 Market St., Suite 202
Lemoyne, PA 17043-1420
(717) 234-5091
(800) 233-9055
*www.rughookingonline.com*
*rughook@paonline.com*

## ABOUT THE PUBLISHER

*Rug Hooking* magazine, the publisher of *Hooked on the Wild Side*, welcomes you to the rug hooking community. Since 1989 *Rug Hooking* has served thousands of rug hookers around the world with its instructional, illustrated articles on dyeing, designing, color planning, hooking techniques, and more. Each issue of the magazine contains color photographs of beautiful rugs old and new, profiles of teachers, designers, and fellow rug hookers, and announcements of workshops, exhibits, and gatherings.

*Rug Hooking* has responded to its readers' demand for more inspiration and information by establishing an inviting, informative web site at *www.rughookingonline.com* and by publishing a number of books on this fiber art. Along with how-to pattern books and a Sourcebook listing of teachers, guilds, and schools, *Rug Hooking* has produced the competition-based book series *A Celebration of Hand-Hooked Rugs*, now in its 14th year. *Hooked on the Wild Side* is part of *Rug Hooking*'s popular Framework Series of in-depth educational books.

The hand-hooked rugs you'll see in *Hooked on the Wild Side* represent just a fragment of the incredible art that is being produced today by women and men of all ages. For more information on rug hooking and *Rug Hooking* magazine, call or write us at the address on page 2.

I f you've ever wondered how to design, draw, and hook an animal that looks realistic but aren't sure where to begin or how to achieve this effect, then this is the book for you.

Learn from the master, Elizabeth Black, affectionately known as the "animal lady", who will guide you step by step through every aspect of creating animals from start to finish. No matter what your preference—cats or dogs, horses, pigs and cows, or wild animals—she provides complete details for hooking the fur and skin, eyes, ears, mouth, and body, so the finished product appears as close to the real animal as possible.

This newest book in our Framework Series, *Hooked on the Wild Side*, will take what seems to be an overwhelming project and turn it into an understandable step-by-step process that can be easily followed. The beautiful examples presented throughout this book will inspire any rug hooker who loves animals and would like to incorporate them into their designs. See how it's done from the first loop to the last and don't be afraid to make mistakes along the way—just tear them out and rework the area. Elizabeth's animals are incredible; they are so lifelike they appear ready to walk off the rug. To achieve this kind of result is well worth the effort.

*The beautiful examples presented throughout this book will inspire any rug hooker who loves animals and would like to incorporate them into their work.*

*Hooked on the Wild Side* includes tips on the importance of well-drawn animals and using visuals, plus advice on what types of backing to use and how to transfer your pattern. The chapter on preparing your project contains dye instruction by Gail Dufresne, who dyes most of the wool for Elizabeth Black's animals. She discusses the use of cold dye solutions to achieve the colors needed and gives formulas for using ordinary household measures instead of special dye implements. Her chart is especially helpful in making conversions from dry-dye to cold-dye solution bottles.

We at *Rug Hooking* magazine hope that this beautifully illustrated step-by-step publication will provide inspiration and further encourage your creative hooking talents.
—*Ginny Stimmel*

*Ginny Stimmel*

## The Evolution of A Rug Hooker

**FOX RUG, 7' x 5', #3-cut wool on rug warp. Designed and hooked by Elizabeth Black, Bentonville, Virginia, 1992.**

*Elizabeth Black*

My long, ongoing adventure with rug hooking started in the mid 1960s, when my 18-month-old daughter "discovered" my oil paints during a time when I was talking on the telephone. She quickly took my brush and added her own strokes to my canvas. The worst part of this scenario was not the loss of the painting, but my daughter's determination to have oils, not a glass of water, to use on her canvas—a large kitchen window—while I used the real thing. It soon became apparent that the best solution was to find another hobby until she was older.

Shortly after reaching this conclusion, I attended a local arts festival and saw an exhibit of hooked rugs. I quickly decided this had definite possibilities—my daughter couldn't eat it, spill it, or harm herself as long as the scissors and hook were out of reach. The woman hosting the exhibit was most helpful in answering my many questions until I announced that I wanted to do my own designs. She quickly informed me that was not allowed, and when I persisted, I was told that either I would hook the existing patterns or I would not be permitted to take lessons. Lessons—who needs lessons? I went to the library, checked out Charlotte Stratton's book, *Rug Hooking Made Easy* [Harper & Row, 1955], and taught myself how to hook.

Those early years were filled with demonstrating the art, juried art and craft shows, several one-woman shows, television and radio, commission work, and some teaching. With my husband's encouragement and help, we also produced a line of patterns.

> *As more of my work focused on animals, my teaching also began to revolve around the animal kingdom.*

Then came the animals. Over the years I hooked a few realistic animals, but I decided to do several pillows of animals to display at a juried show. They all quickly sold. People were soon commissioning me to do their pets or favorite animals.

As more of my work focused on animals, my teaching also began to revolve around the animal kingdom. Hence I became affectionately, I hope, known as the "animal lady." With a title like that, how could I not write a book on hooking animals? The book is finished, but not my passion for hooking. It's been a fascinating journey that has brought many wonderful people into my life throughout the years, whose friendships are deeply cherished.

My heartfelt thanks to all of you who encouraged me to write *Hooked on the Wild Side* and make it a reality.
—*Elizabeth Black*

# WHAT IS RUG HOOKING?

Some strips of wool. A simple tool. A bit of burlap. How ingenious were the women and men of ages past to see how such humble household items could make such beautiful rugs?

Although some form of traditional rug hooking has existed for centuries, this fiber craft became a fiber art only in the last 150 years. The fundamental steps have remained the same: A pattern is drawn onto a foundation, such as burlap or linen. A zigzag line of stitches is sewn along the foundation's edges to keep them from fraying as the rug is worked. The foundation is then stretched onto a frame, and fabric strips or yarn, which may have been dyed by hand, are pulled through it with an implement that resembles a crochet hook inserted into a wooden handle. The compacted loops of wool remain in place without knots or stitching. The completed rug may have its edges whipstitched with cording and yarn as a finishing touch to add durability.

Despite the simplicity of the basic method, highly intricate designs can be created with it. Using a multitude of dyeing techniques to produce unusual effects, or various hooking methods to create realistic shading, or different widths of wool to achieve a primitive or formal style, today's rug hookers have gone beyond making strictly utilitarian floor coverings to also make wallhangings, vests, lampshades, purses, pictorials, portraits, and more. Some have incorporated other kinds of needlework into their hooked rugs to fashion unique and fascinating fiber art that's been shown in museums, exhibits, and galleries throughout the world.

For a good look at what contemporary rug hookers are doing with yesteryear's craft—or to learn how to hook your own rug—pick up a copy of *Rug Hooking* magazine, or visit our web site at www.rughookingonline.com. Within the world of rug hooking—and *Rug Hooking* magazine—you'll find there's a style to suit every taste and a growing community of giving, gracious fiber artists who will welcome you to their gatherings.—*Ginny Stimmel*

# CHAPTER 1

# PREPARING YOUR PROJECT

INSIDE THE ARK, *60" x 36", #2 and 3-cut wool on rug warp. Designed and hooked by Elizabeth Black, Bentonville, Virginia, 1998.*

## The Importance of a Well-Drawn Animal

One of the most important elements to address in the early stages of your project is how to create a very well drawn animal (or animals). If this fundamental part of the design is out of proportion and poorly executed you will not end up with the successful piece that you have envisioned.

I find that working from a good visual makes the drawing process much easier. If your own pet is used as the subject, take some photos—preferably in a pose similar to the one that you plan to use in the design—and use one of these as a visual. If the subject is not your own pet, do some research to find a good photo of the animal you plan to feature in the design. (Once again, choose a photo featuring the animal in a pose similar to what you plan to use.)

Another option is to take a photo and have it enlarged on either a copy machine or an overhead-enlarging machine. Increase the photo to the correct size for the project. If you are using a copyrighted photo, drawing, painting, etc., be sure to contact the copyright holder for permission to use their artwork.

If you are not familiar with the Dover Book Publications, you are missing out on a great and vast design resource! Dover prints soft cover books featuring drawings, photos, and designs of just about every subject imaginable and many of the designs, drawings, and photos are free to use without permission. These publications are very reasonably priced and can be very useful to the "drawing challenged" individual. (Catalogs of Dover's entire selection of books can be obtained by visiting their web site at http://store.doverpublications.com/)

## TIP: DRAWING STRATEGY

Don't be discouraged if your ability to draw leaves much to be desired, as there are several options that can be explored; ask a friend who has some drawing ability to help, or pay an artisan to draw the animal.

## Visuals

If you aren't accustomed to using visuals, I would strongly urge you to start working with them. Visuals are wonderful tools to aid in the creation of a true likeness of the subject matter. We all know what a cow or a giraffe looks like ...at least we assume that we do, but do we really know the color of their eyes and the length of their tail? Are lions really gold and tigers really orange?

These are but two examples of why a good visual of the animal about to be hooked is so important. The visual will serve as a guide for proportion, muscle structure, color, and shading. Ideally, using just one visual is best or at least try limiting the visuals to not more than two. Each visual will vary in color and shading according to the light conditions present at the time the photo was taken. It's a good idea to have a color copy as well as a black and white copy of the visual. The black and white copy will give additional definition to the shaded areas. Also, choose a visual that is in a similar pose, facing the same direction as the drawing.

If the animal in the visual is too small, enlarge the portion that you wish to use. This will enable you to view more clearly and in detail, the subtle changes of color and the various directions in which the fur or hair grows.

## Backing

Backing is extremely important, as it is the foundation of your piece. Also, consider if what you have chosen will survive and endure years of use without requiring major repair. My personal preference is cotton backing, which is referred to as "rug warp" or "duck" cloth. This cloth is milled specifi-

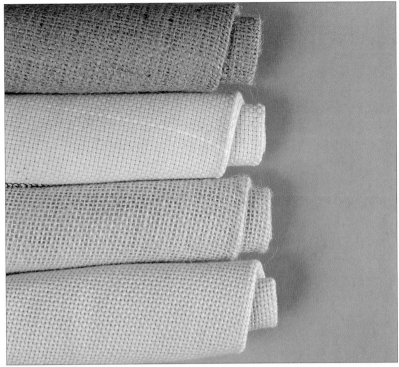

TOP TO BOTTOM: *burlap, monk's cloth, linen, rug warp*

### TIP: THE PERFECT CUT

Before cutting a piece of the backing, take a pencil and mark off the size that you wish to cut. Run a bead of Elmer's White Glue along each of the pencil lines. Next take something stiff, such as a small piece of cardboard or a credit card, and spread the glue evenly over the pencil lines. Let dry (when dry the glue will become completely clear and smooth). Once the glue is dry, take scissors and cut out the fabric on the pencil lines. This method seals the edges of the backing and will eliminate the need to stitch the edges on a sewing machine.

cally for rug work. Warp or duck cloth in relatively small amounts can be purchased from numerous rug hooking suppliers; larger amounts can be purchased directly from one of the mills that produces it. (Southern Mills of Union City, Georgia is one that I use.) It is evenly woven; a nice off-white in color and it retains its shape. A straight line can easily be drawn just by following the weave of the fabric. The rug warp will work well up through a #5 cut blade. Beyond that it may be too difficult to pull your strips through the backing.

My second choice for backing is

linen. There are a wide variety of linens available for both fine and wide-cut projects. If you are working in a narrow cut be sure it is woven closely enough to hold your strips. Try several different linen backings until you find one that meets your requirements.

Some people are very satisfied with monk's cloth, but I find that it stretches too much and doesn't lend itself to narrow cuts.

My last choice for backing is burlap. I don't feel that it offers the durability of warp cloth and linen and it isn't as pleasing to work on.

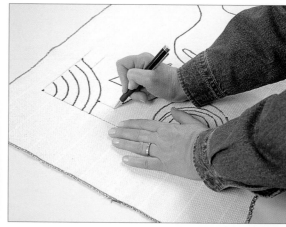

## Transferring Your Pattern

Before transferring the design onto the backing, do a master drawing of the entire piece. Make sure the placement of all of the design elements is exactly the way that you want them. The following is the method I have used for many years to transfer my patterns:

■ Lay your master drawing on a flat surface and take a piece of very sheer material such as Red Dot, or interfacing for silk, and cut it to cover the surface of your master drawing. Once the fabric is lined up properly, weigh it down so it cannot move around or shift. (I use drafting weights, but anything heavy such as canned goods or books will work.)

■ Take a Sanford Sharpie pen and trace all the lines from your master drawing onto the transfer fabric. Once you've done that, remove the fabric from the drawing and put your master drawing aside.

■ Lay the backing cut to the proper size on a flat surface. Place the transfer fabric (onto which the design has been drawn) over the backing material, making sure that it is correctly aligned. Pin it to the backing, using enough pins to keep it from shifting.

■ Trace the design from the transfer fabric onto the backing material, using a Sanford Rub-a-Dub black marking pen. This pen is designed to be used on fiber; (a regular Sharpie is not). Rub-a-Dub pens are available at almost any store that carries office or art supplies.

■ Using your Rub-a-Dub marker, trace over all the lines previously drawn onto the sheer transfer fabric. By doing this, the ink from the marker will flow through the fabric and will mark the backing material to transfer the design (be sure to use enough pressure while tracing to create a dark line on the backing.)

■ Once all of the lines on the transfer fabric have been traced onto the backing, remove the pins and the transfer fabric from the backing. Now check the backing to make sure that all the lines on the final transfer are dark enough. If there are faint lines, touch them up with the Sharpie pen to darken them. Save your master drawing and transfer fabric for future use.

## Selecting the Wool

All the wool used should be of good quality. If recycled wool is used, make sure it has been washed and is moth-free. Over the years I have discovered that animals are most easily created by using a combination of the following types of wool:

### TIP: TIME WELL SPENT

Don't be in a hurry to transfer your design! In fact, view it a number of times over the course of several days to be sure you are satisfied with the overall look. If not satisfied, work on it some more. Believe me, this will be time well spent, as often we become so enthused with an idea, that we forget to slow down and develop it to its fullest potential.

■ **SPOT DYES:** If a strand of hair is pulled from an animal and examined closely, chances are there would be several colors and variations of color all on that single shaft of hair. The overall color seen in an animal's coat, is actually a build up of color, consisting of multi-layers of hair, which gives the coat its final overall color hue. When hooked, spot dyes create a mottled or multi-colored look that mimics the multi-hued color of fur.

■ **DIP DYES:** In some long haired animals, sections of fur go from a dark to a light shade or vice versa (an example of this can be seen on collies). By choosing a dip dye in the appropriate shades this ongoing change of color can be created effortlessly, and it will look very natural.

■ **SOLID COLOR:** Many times I find a solid color is needed as a shadow or definition line in conjunction with my spot or dip dyes.

■ **TEXTURES:** Textures seem like a logical choice to achieve the multi-colored, multi-layered look that we are striving to duplicate. However, many textured fabrics do not cut very well in a narrow cut application. Before deciding to include textures in the piece try cutting them with a #3 or #4 cut blade. Don't assume they will work until a few strands have been cut and hooking has been tried hooking with them. If working in a wider cut than a #3 or #4, they may work very well in the piece and give the look that you want.

■ **SWATCHES:** Swatches can be used, but I find that they do not give the fur-like look that I can achieve with the other types of dyed wool.

As you experiment with a combination of the various selections, I am confi-

dent that you will find the right "mix" to accomplish the desired look.

## Dyeing Wool for Animals

Those of you who are familiar with my work have adjusted to the fact that I don't do any dyeing. The rest of you are probably wondering how I've hooked for so many years without entering into the world of dye pots. When I first taught myself to hook I found it a challenge to find sources for the basic items that I needed. I didn't want to use stamped patterns so I chose to spend what extra time I had designing my own

pieces and purchasing wool. Whenever I see wool that 'speaks to me' I buy it and add it to my ever-growing stash, knowing that sometime in the future I will use it.

Besides buying what appeals to me, I have been very fortunate to have friends such as Maryanne Lincoln, Maxine Gallagher, and Gail Dufresne who have patiently listened to the description of what I want and have created this formula in their dye pots. Their expertise has also made it possible for me to continually replenish my supply of certain colors that have become part of my basic palette for hooking animals.

# A DIFFERENT WAY TO DYE

*by Gail Dufresne*

## Dyeing by Eye and Visual Aids

Many of us are crazy about our pets (like me!) and want to capture the look of these critters in our realistic hooking. The most effective way to match a pet's colors is to dye from a photograph or by direct observation. Once you learn how to do this, anything can be dyed in this manner to get the desired look. Some general formulas are provided as examples, but as you teach yourself to dye by eye, your very own dyeing combinations will soon be discovered.

Elizabeth never uses swatches. (Swatches are several very close values the same color, typically 6-to-8 different shades.) She prefers to use dip dyes (wool dipped in dye), over-dyes (wool immersed in a dye bath), and spot dyes. The method described here is spot dyeing, which is wool that has been scrunched in a pan and spotted or mottled with dye.

About the same time that I began dyeing for Elizabeth, I switched to dyeing with solution bottles. I was interested in having my dyes all set up and ready to use rather than having to mix dyes from scratch each time I wanted to dye. Once the bottles were made up and cooled, I would be dealing with cold dye solutions, which reduces my exposure to boiling water and the more harmful, dry dyes.

With this method I can get very small amounts of dye using a regular kitchen-measuring spoon, not a special dye spoon. With this system, as you can see by **FIGURE 1**, 1 teaspoon of dry dye measure equals 2 cups of wet dye solution; $^1/_2$ teaspoon of dry dye measure equals 1 cup of wet dye. Continuing down **FIGURE 1**, $^1/_{128}$ teaspoon

| FIGURE 1 | | | |
|---|---|---|---|
| **Dry Dye** | **Wet Dye Solution** | | |
| Measure | Cups | tbs | tsp |
| 1 tsp | 2 | 32 | 96 |
| $^1/_2$ tsp | 1 | 16 | 48 |
| $^1/_4$ tsp | $^1/_2$ | 8 | 24 |
| $^1/_8$ tsp | $^1/_4$ | 4 | 12 |
| $^1/_{16}$ tsp | $^1/_8$ | 2 | 6 |
| $^1/_{32}$ tsp | $^1/_{16}$ | 1 | 3 |
| $^1/_{64}$ tsp | $^1/_{32}$ | $^1/_2$ | 1 $^1/_2$ |
| $^1/_{128}$ tsp | $^1/_{64}$ | $^1/_4$ | $^3/_4$ |

of dry dye measure is equal to $^3/_4$ teaspoon of wet dye solution. A special dye spoon is not needed at all! One can get $^1/_{256}$ of a teaspoon of dry dye measure by using $^3/_8$ teaspoon of the wet solution. The last three columns of **FIGURE 1** are conversions between the three different measurement units.

## Dyeing Solutions

I almost always use one of four PRO Chem wash-fast acid dyes: #119 yellow, #338 red, #490 blue, and #672 black. I switched from using just the primary dyes because I learned more about color and dyeing if I mixed all my dyes from the primaries, not from premixed formulas where most of the work has already been done for me.

I squish a full yard of soaked wool into a 12"deep by 20" long by 12" wide stainless steel pan. Then using light plastic gloves (no need for heavy gloves with cold dye solutions), I paint the wool while looking at some sort of visual aid; pieces of wool I am trying to match, or a photograph, for example. Working the dye solution in with my hand results in a much more thorough dye absorption than any other method I have used.

I practiced dyeing by eye by finding things to paint—like skies from post cards that I really like, ocean water from a painting, flowers from a book or photograph—inspiration can be found everywhere. I dye for Elizabeth's students by looking at photographs of the animals they will be hooking.

One of the most valuable lessons learned is to be able to hook what I see, and I have found in my own teaching that it is a very hard concept for many to grasp.

It is absolutely *not* true that either one is or is not born with a good sense of color. It can be learned and you don't need to be dependent on a color wheel. A color wheel is almost never used to color plan my work or my student's work. Dye formulas are rarely used anymore, except for a few of my own.

At the risk of creating confusion, I have given as much information as I can about my method of dyeing, because it is a wonderful system and so many of my students now use it. Be that as it may, I have given dry dye formulas, not wet dye solutions amounts here, because many of you may not want to switch to my system. Use the formulas here as you would any formula from a dye book now on the market. If you are using my dye system you will want to

### TIP: DYE-BY-EYE

Most people have a far better color sense than they think they do, and through dyeing, especially if you get away from the formula books and trust your own eye, that sense can be fine-tuned.

convert these formulas into wet dye solution amounts by referring to the conversion table in **FIGURE 1**.

## Types of Wool

Most (but not all) textures cannot be used for realistic fine cut animals hooked in a #3 or #4 cut, as they will fray when cut in strips that narrow. Cashmere and camel hair are wonderful to use because they are soft and luxurious, like fur, and will not fall apart in narrower cuts. Some folks don't like to use these softer and potentially less durable fibers, but I love to use them and will worry about it later if they don't hold up. The areas could always be rehooked and the fabrics add so much to the final work that it is worth the risk. They can often be found in colors perfect for animals: camel, gray, brown, and black. If unsure of the stability of wool that you would like to use, test it first by cutting it to see if it will fall apart.

FIGURE 2, *white animal swatches*

## Different Types of Animals by Color

Animals can be broken down into several color categories. There are, for instance, white animals, gray animals, and black animals. Dyeing for all of these are the same—use black dye! I find PRO Chem #672 black or Majic Carpet Black best to use.

■ **WHITE AMIMALS:** Here is where some rules are broken and undyed white can be used as the lightest value, or highlight. You will then need at least two darker shades of white. The second value could be an undyed natural, or a white that is not as white as the highlight wool. The third wool is for shadows, which can be accomplished by using a *very small* amount ($1/128$ tsp or less over a yard) of PRO Chem #672 black or Majic Carpet Black over white or natural wool. Squish a full yard of presoaked natural or white wool into the stainless steel dye pan as discussed above and then add a very small amount of pre-mixed dye into a 4-cup measure, fill the cup with water, and slowly pour onto the wool. Work the solution into the wool with your hands. (Remember to use light gloves.) If it needs to be darker simply add more black dye in very small increments until satisfied. The value can be determined by looking at the visual aid while dyeing the wool. Remember that the wool will be quite a bit lighter after it is washed and dried.

FIGURE 3, *Elizabeth Black's Black swatches*

I stockpile lots of this wool by hand painting in the above manner with $1/128$ tsp, $1/64$ tsp, $1/32$ tsp, $1/16$ tsp, $1/8$ tsp, and $1/4$ tsp of PRO Chem #672 black. I start with white, natural, or tan wool. These formulas are all you need to prepare wool for most animals. See **FIGURE 2**.

■ **BLACK ANIMALS:** For a black animal use undyed black and move into a dark gray for highlights. Dorr Mills sells black wool by special order that was made especially for Elizabeth called Elizabeth Black's Black. This wool has a decidedly brown cast. Gorgeous mottled black wool can be achieved by dyeing over dark brown or gray wool. **FIGURE 3** shows examples of Elizabeth Black's Black, a brown mottled with black, and an undyed black. I use several different brown and gray wools, including cashmere and camel hair. Squish a full yard of soaked natural, gray, or black into the pan and work in a full teaspoon of black, or even more, depending on how dark the wool needs to be. You may need to move into a dark gray for the highlights. This can be achieved in the same manner as the shadow wool for white animals. The amount depends on the value of the highlights. Look at the visual aid while dyeing the wool and see how dark the fur is, then dye what you see, keeping in mind that wet wool is several values darker than dry wool.

■ **GRAY ANIMALS:** For a gray animal use undyed gray wools and move from there into an undyed black for the shadows. I use several different natural, white, black, and gray wools, including cashmere and camel hair. Squish a full yard of soaked natural, gray, or black wool into the dye pan and work it up to a full teaspoon of black, depending on how dark the wool needs to be. Highlights can be achieved in the same manner as the shadow wool for white animals. Spot dye natural or white wool with black. The amount depends on how light the highlights should be. Look at the visual aid while dyeing the wool and dye what you see. Again, wet wool is several values darker than dry wool.

■ **BROWN ANIMALS:** Tan and brown wool spotted with black or brown is great for many brown animals. I usually make up my own brown using the primaries (red, blue, and yellow). Mix them together using more yellow (the weakest of the three dyes), less red than yellow, and the least blue (the strongest). Once brown is achieved, use more yellow for a yellow brown, more red for a red brown, etc. Using just the primaries and relying on your eye to get the right color is the best way to learn about color and dyeing by eye. Also, one of several great Cushing browns could be used; Medium brown and Golden brown are both good browns.

■ **LIONS AND GOLDEN RETRIEVERS:** It was difficult to come up with a formula I like for these guys, so I "cheated." When I first took the time to learn how to dye by eye and only use primary colors, I tried to convert all of my favorite formulas from Cushing dyes (which is what I used when I first learned to dye) to PRO Chem dyes. This was one that I could not beat. I set up a 16-ounce solution bottle with $^1/_4$ teaspoon each of Cushing

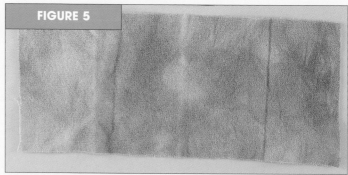

FIGURE 5, *animal tongue swatches*

Champagne, Ecru, and Old Ivory. I call it "Onions." I then use it like any other color in one of my solution bottles. It is perfect for a lion or a golden retriever. I use it to dye over white, natural, cream, tan, and camel. Using all of these wools should give all the values needed for a good-looking lion. If not, try a little Cushing Golden Brown over any of those wools for the darker shadows.

■ **TIGERS, FOXES AND IRISH SETTERS:** A good formula for tigers is $^1/_4$ tsp PRO Chem yellow #119, $^1/_{16}$ tsp PRO Chem red #338, and $^1/_{32}$ tsp PRO Chem black #672 over 1 yard wool. For different values of the same color, simply double or halve the amounts. Doubling or quadrupling the formula makes it redder and great for red foxes and Irish setters. Adjustments may need to be made to

FIGURE 4, *brown animal swatches*

get the exact colors for your particular critter. See **FIGURE 4** for a good-looking tiger, which uses undyed white, white spot dyed with $^1/_{64}$ tsp PRO Chem black #672 over 1 yard white, $^1/_8$ tsp of my Cushing "Onions" formula (described in Lions and Golden Retrievers), one piece of the tiger formula I mentioned above, and two pieces of the tiger formula quadrupled to get colors for wool that would work well for Irish setters and red foxes.

■ **ANIMAL TONGUES ARE NOT PINK:** A formula for a realistic animal tongue is $^1/_{128}$ tsp PRO Chem yellow #119, $^1/_{128}$ tsp + $^1/_{256}$ tsp PRO Chem red #338, $^1/_{128}$ tsp PRO Chem black #672 over 1 yard of white or natural wool. Okay, I cheated again, but caramel is a great, relatively new dye. I worked for a long time to get a good tongue color and I think this works pretty well. See **FIGURE 5**. Again, this is only a guide. The formula may need to be adjusted to work with your animal.

# CHAPTER 2

# FUR AND SKIN

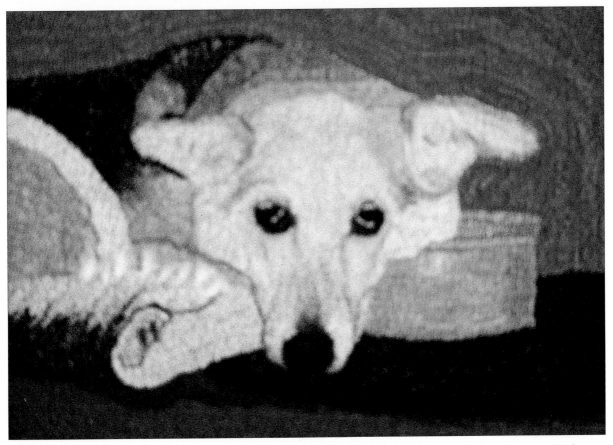

*WAITING FOR DINNER, 18" x 17", #3- and 4-cut wool on rug warp. Designed by Elizabeth Black. Hooked by Barbara Personette, Fairfax, Virginia, 2003.*

On longhaired animals, both domestic and wild, the surface color seen is a combination of the various shades of color that appear on each individual shaft of hair. Layers of color cannot be built up when working with wool as it can when painting. The only way to achieve this illusion is by carefully selecting the necessary wool. If there are areas of fur that run from dark to light, a dip dye in the appropriate shades would be a good choice. A combination of spot dyes and solid color may be the best solution for sections that appear to be mottled with adjoining areas of solid color. Try using textures in areas that have a very multi-colored look but be sure they will cut in the width needed and that they will not fall apart when hooked. In order to achieve the desired effect use wool that has been dyed in various ways along with a swatch or bolt wool.

Before hooking fur or hair check the visual carefully to determine what direction it is growing. Don't be surprised to find it growing in different directions on various parts of the animal. Directional hooking is what helps to give your animal shape and dimension so it is very important to hook in the same direction that the hair or fur appears to lie.

## TIP: DIRECTIONAL HOOKING

I find it helpful to take my Rub-a-Dub marker and draw lines on my pattern duplicating the direction that the fur or hair lies. These lines will help guide toward hooking in the proper direction.

## Long Hair

Longhaired animals have multiple layers of fur. Hook the top layer first and progress down through the various layers. For example, the chest on a collie or longhaired cat is often viewed as several layers with the top layer being the section directly under the chin. About halfway down the chest this layer will end and a second layer will begin.

Always observe each area about to be hooked, then break it down into layers, and hook layer-by-layer starting with the top. Hook each layer in the direction in which the fur appears to be growing.

## Short Hair

The form and structure is more visible in shorthaired animals. However, just as in longhaired subjects, the hair does appear to go in various directions. Once again it is very important to study the visual and hook the hair or fur in the direction in which it grows. By doing this, bone structure and muscular areas can be defined, which will help give your animal dimension. Generally, I rely on spot dyes and solid color for shorthaired animals.

## Skin

Sometimes there are areas found on animals that resemble skin more than fur or hair (good examples of this are some monkey and giraffe faces). To duplicate these sections I use very subtle spot dyes and solid color always hooking in the direction that will give form and definition to the area.

*RIGHT: Close-up of PIGTORIAL, 40" x 30", #3-cut wool on rug warp. Designed and hooked by Elizabeth Black, Bentonville, Virginia, 1999.*

*COCO, 14 1/2" x 22 1/2", #3-cut wool on wool backing. Designed and hooked by Liz Marino, South Egremont, Massachusetts, 2000.*

POSITION ALERT, 25" x 20", #3 and 4-cut wool on rug warp. Designed by Elizabeth Black. Hooked by Kay Weeks, Port Murray, New Jersey, 2000.

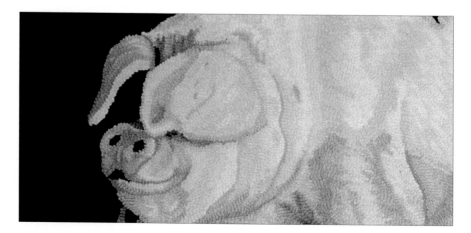

# CHAPTER 3

# FACES

*JAGUAR PILLOW, 20" x 20", #3-cut wool on rug warp. Designed and hooked by Elizabeth Black, Bentonville, Virginia, 1993.*

O ver the years I have discovered that the easiest and most successful way to hook an animal is to follow a series of steps, similar to the pieces of a jigsaw puzzle. I start with several pieces and keep adding to them until the design is completed.

The first piece of the design is the face. Before beginning to hook, study the face on the visual closely to become familiar with anything that makes it unique. Each animal, just as with people, varies in appearance.

## Eyes

T he first area of the face to concentrate on is the eyes, but before hooking begins, be sure that they are correctly positioned, approximately the same size, and the proper shape.

Hook the outline around the eye duplicating the shape that you see on the visual. This outline can be one or more dark rows depending on the size of the eye.

*Parts of the eye*

*Two types of domestic cat eyes*

The eyes are the "soul" of the animal and to give them life they must each have a highlight. (Without that spark of life I'm afraid you would end up with the equivalent of road kill!)

Hook the highlight in the eye first using a strip of white wool. If the eye is very small use a strip cut with a #2 blade. Hook the strip through the backing bringing the two ends up next to each other (there won't be a loop between the two ends). Cut each end

15

off leaving a tail on each that is approximately $\frac{1}{2}$" long. For a larger eye follow the same procedure using a #3-cut strip. For a very large eye, an end, one loop and an end may be wanted. Don't trim off the ends at this time.

After hooking the highlight, hook the area immediately around it or next to it depending on where the highlight is positioned. This is usually the pupil and it is almost always dark brown or black. Check the visual for color and shape and duplicate as seen. (This will be hooked with either a strip cut on a #2 or #3 cut blade depending on the size of the pupil.)

tails of the highlight tightly together. Hold them twisted together with one hand and cut them off to the same height as the loops in the completed pupil. Repeat this procedure on the second eye.

desired shade and hook one or more rows around the pupil. Cut and start again with a lighter section of the strand and hook at least one more row. Adjust the number of rows hooked depending on the size of the eye. The other option you have is to pull several shades out of an appropriate swatch and follow the same procedure. For some reason the first choice of color for the iris often looks too washed out or dull after it is hooked. To avoid this, choose a brighter or more intense color for this area. Some animals have a subtle tinge of red surrounding the iris. If this is seen in the eye, substitute a beige

---

*"The eyes are the 'soul' of the animal and to give them life they must each have a highlight."*

---

If the pupil appears to be round or oval in shape hook the appropriate number of rows or partial rows to duplicate what is seen on the visual. If the pupil is more elongated as it is in some animals, (various breeds of cats fall in this category), hook it in a vertical direction next to or around the highlight. Again, hook the number of rows or partial rows needed to achieve the correct size pupil.

Once the pupil is hooked twist the two

Now that the pupil is hooked, study the adjoining section of the eye, the iris. The iris surrounds the pupil and can be a variety of colors. If the iris appears to be multi-flecked in color, a spot dye combining the appropriate shades works well. The iris may also appear to consist of two rings of color directly around the pupil changing to another shade as it progresses outward. In this case try using a dip dye in the appropriate shades. Pull the dip-dyed strip to the

pink or something similar. (If it's too red or pink your animal will look like he has an eye infection and is waiting to see the vet!)

Take a look at the completed eye. Does it capture the color and shape seen in the visual? Is there a small area within the outline that needs to be filled in with some color? If so, choose a pale beige or ivory and this will fill in but not give a wild look to the eye, unless that's the look you wanted; in that case, use white.

Now that one eye has been successfully completed and you are pleased with the outcome, go ahead and do the other eye while all the proper shades are in front of you.

## TIP: EYES THAT SHINE

Take a pen and mark one highlight in each eye. Try to position them just as they appear on the visual. By marking them on the pattern you can immediately tell if they are in the right place and avoid having a cross-eyed creature! (Note: Sometimes, if the head is turned and just a small portion of one eye is seen, that eye may not have a highlight.)

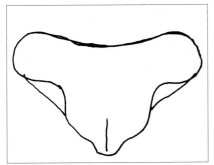

*Basic cat nose*

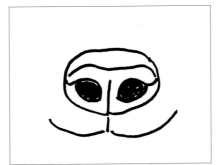

*Basic dog nose*

## Noses

Noses vary a great deal in size, shape, and color. Once again refer to the visual as a guide. Before choosing the color, check to see if the nose is drawn in the correct shape and size.

◼ CAT'S NOSE: As seen in the example, a cat's nose is oddly shaped. Also note how the nostrils often look like they are almost part of the outline of the nose. Keep in mind cats' noses are usually a small area on the face. Because of this, keep them as simple as possible showing only the basic structure and not a lot of detail.

to make them too large!

On many cats there is a dark line that begins at the base of the nose and proceeds up through the nose as a vertical line. It usually stops about $^3/_4$ of the way up the nose (notice how it often stops even with the top of the nostrils), but check the visual for the correct length. Hook this line in the proper color and shade. If there is an area at the base of the nose on each side of the line just completed, approximately the same color as the line, hook these sections now. (This area is all inside the outline of the nose.) If there are any spots or odd markings on

If a highlight on the nose is seen, hook it at this time. It usually appears near the top of the nose and is often curved. Hook the highlight in a shade lighter than the rest of the nose. (The color should vary from the rest of the nose but not be distracting.)

The remaining portion of the nose will usually be in several shades of black and gray. If using pinks, unless they are very pale in your visual, tone them down. No one wants a neon light in the middle of the cat's face! Consider a subtle pink spot dye, several solid shades of pink or a combination of the two to complete the nose.

◼ DOG'S NOSE: Just as with cats, the size, shape, and color of the nose can vary from one breed to another. Look at the visual and study the nose.

Proceed by hooking the outline of the nose using the proper color or colors. Hooking the outline will help keep the correct shape and reduces the chances of it "growing".

---

*"The goal is to acknowledge that the nostrils exist without them becoming a focal point. Be careful not to make them too large!"*

---

Outline the nose in the color or colors seen on the visual. This outline helps define the shape and keeps the nose from "growing" too large as it is hooked. After completing the outline, decide whether a loop or two for each nostril needs to be added, or if the variation in color is enough to define the nostrils. If the nostrils are positioned in the face and not on the outline hook them now. The goal is to acknowledge that the nostrils exist without them becoming a focal point. Be careful not

the remaining portion of the nose do these now in the correct colors and tones. Fill in the rest of the nose with the previously selected pinks.

If the nose is dark, follow the same procedure; outline, nostrils, vertical line, highlight, and fill the remainder of the nose with the correct shades. When using black for the outline, nostrils and vertical line, fill the remainder of the nose with Dorr's Elizabeth Black's Black. If black looks too harsh, substitute shades of gray.

After completing the outline check the size and shape of the nostrils and then hook them. They are usually black or brown in color. Take care not to make them too large. In fact, I often downsize them a small amount. Nostrils need to be acknowledged as part of the nose but not as a focal point.

If a dark line is seen that begins at the base of the nose and proceeds up through the center of the nose as a vertical line, hook this line in the proper shade. This line visually divides approxi-

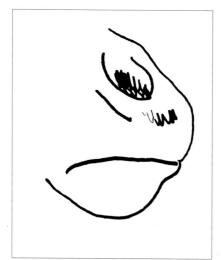

*Horse muzzle profile*

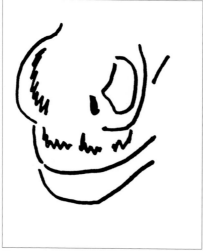

*Horse muzzle*

*Pig snout*

mately the bottom ³/₄ of the nose but refer to the visual for the right length. (Note how it often stops even with the top line of the nostrils.)

Many times at least one highlight on a dog's nose will be seen. This will often appear as a curved line near the top of the nose inside your outline. To hook this, choose a shade somewhat lighter than the color you use in the remainder of the nose. Example—black nose: Use black for nostrils and outline and use Elizabeth Black's Black to fill.

The choice for the highlight should be a shade of gray that creates a subtle contrast from the shades of black. Don't use white or too light a shade for the highlight. If your eye immediately goes to the highlight once the nose is completed, there is too much of a contrast.

This highlight often consists of one row and a partial row, depending on the size of the nose. The partial row helps to keep the highlight from looking like just one stripe of color. If the nose is mottled in color (such as a combination of blacks and grays or browns), a spot dye works well instead of the second color originally chosen to fill in the nose area.

**HORSE'S NOSE:** The nose on a horse is actually part of the area referred to as the muzzle (the upper lip, lower lip, and chin). Hook the basic outline of the nostril paying close attention to the shape. Duplicate it as closely as possible. Hook the section that appears to be a rim on the upper portion of the nostril. Continue by hooking any rim seen on the lower portion of the nostril. This will connect to the just hooked section and will form the front and lower portion of the nostril. Fill the inner section of the nostril starting with the lightest shades and continuing to the darkest. The area surrounding the nostril will be treated as part of the muzzle. (A pale pink spot dye for this area will create a natural mottled appearance.) If the nose has a combination of pink, gray, white, or beige try a spot dye incorporating the colors seen. A dark nose will still have a variation of color. Again try a spot dye or combination of straight color along with a spot dye to get the subtle changes seen in the visual.

**PIG'S NOSE:** I find it difficult to look at a pig without having the urge to smile. They definitely have a personality, and yes, some even have an attitude. Pigs are

a challenge to hook for a number of reasons and finding the proper shades of color heads the list. But for now I'll stick to the subject of their nose (or to be more anatomically correct—their snout!)

As with the other noses I have discussed, hook the outline of the pig's nose first, being careful to retain the proper shape. (The area referred to is actually the end of the snout, not the bridge portion of the nose.) Next, study the nostrils and hook the outer edge of the nostrils as they appear in the visual. Fill the inner portion of the nostril with the proper color. (Two shades may be needed, one for the shadow, and a second lighter shade for the remaining area inside the nostril.) Continue by hooking any highlights seen on this part of the nose. If they curve, be sure to hook them in a curved direction just as they appear on the visual.

The remainder of the end of the snout is likely to be a combination of various shades of pink. A spot dye is often the easiest way to accomplish this mottled look. (A word of caution—if once it's hooked, the completed section resembles a neon sign causing the eye to immediately focus on this area, it's too bright. Rework it and soften the color.)

Once this portion of the nose is

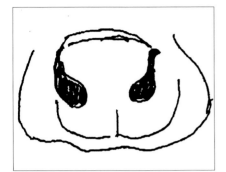

*Cow muzzle front view*

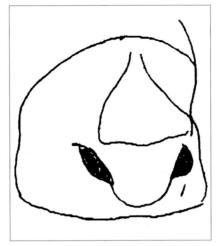

*Cow muzzle ³/4 view*

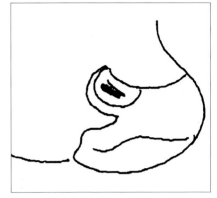

*Cow muzzle side view*

completed, hook the remaining section, which is the bridge. Hook in any light or dark lines or areas seen, taking care to hook them in the same direction seen on the visual. Fill the rest of the nose with the chosen colors, again always working in the direction in which the hair appears to grow.

■ **COW'S NOSE:** Cows' noses are large and oddly shaped and they appear to cover most of the lower section of the face. Check the drawing or pattern to be sure the structure of the nose is a good likeness to what is seen in the visual.

Hook the outline of the nose area, then the outline of the nostrils, being careful to duplicate the shape seen on the visual. Next finish the inner section of the nostrils using the appropriate colors. If a band of color surrounding or partially surrounding the nostrils is seen, complete this next. Proceed by hooking any vertical line seen running from the base of the nose up between the nostrils. Once that is completed, finish all the remaining area between the nostrils in appropriate shades. This area will probably be hooked vertically and run from the lip line, up between the nostrils to approximately the top of the nostrils. (Check the visual.) Continue by filling in the remainder of the nose area always hooking in the direction in which the hair appears to grow. Again,

several spot dyes may be used to achieve the subtle change of color that is seen on the nose.

■ **NOSES ON OTHER DOMESTIC ANIMALS:** If the nose closely resembles that of one of the animals I have specifically mentioned, use those directions as a guide. Otherwise follow the basic procedure

used; outline the nose, hook the nostrils, then complete any line of color appearing between the nostrils. Continue by hooking any highlights seen on the nose and then fill in the remainder of the nose with the appropriate combination of color. (Spot-dyes are a good choice if a subtle variation of color is needed to complete the nose.)

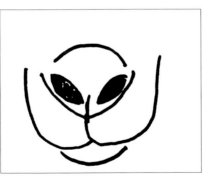

*Domestic sheep frontal*

*Domestic sheep profile*

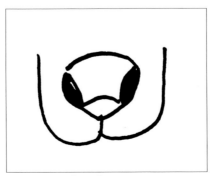

*Domestic goat frontal*

*Domestic goat profile*

## Mouths

People have a tendency to make the mouth line on animals too wide or too short. There is an easy way to check to see if this line is the correct length before starting to hook. Take the visual and lay a strand of wool at the outer edge of the mouth line and run the strand upwards until it intersects the eye. (Is it intersecting near the center of the eye or the outer edge of the eye?) Now take a strand of wool and repeat the procedure on the pattern. Immediately see if the outer edges of the mouth on the pattern intersect the eye in approximately the same place as they do on the visual. If needed adjust the length of the line.

■ **CAT'S MOUTH:** A cat's mouth is quite simple. Look carefully at the visual and notice a short vertical line running down from the center of the base of the nose to the mouth. This line connects the nose and the mouth. Hook this line duplicating the color seen on the visual, then the mouth line taking care not to make it too dark unless it is a dark line. (On some felines the line will be very subtle in color and barely visible.) Also, be careful not to hook the corners of the mouth in a downward slant unless an unhappy looking creature is wanted. If a second, very short partial

row directly under the mouth line is seen, finish those few loops now.

■ **DOG'S MOUTH:** Before beginning, again look at the mouth on the visual. What is really there? Is it a very long droopy line such as seen in hounds, or is it straight across and small like a Pomeranian? Getting this line the proper shape and length is the key to shaping the lower part of the face. Take lots of time and be sure that the lines on the pattern correspond with those on the visual. (Use the same method outlined for the cat's mouth to check proportions.)

In many breeds (such as hounds and bulldogs) the mouth line appears to continue in a downward curve that forms the inner line and shape of the jowls. If this is the case continue this line to duplicate what is seen on the visual.

If the dog's mouth is open, the lower mouth line may have an irregular shape. Try to duplicate this as closely as possible to resemble what is on the visual.

First let's discuss the mouth in a closed position. Just as on cats, many breeds of dogs have a visible vertical line that starts at the center of the base of the nose and connects the nose and the mouth line. This line appears to divide the lower part of the face and is usually the same shade as the mouth line. After this vertical line is hooked, proceed to the mouth line. One line for the mouth may not be enough so add a second row or partial second row to

duplicate what is seen on the visual. These lines are usually a dark shade.

When the mouth is open an additional area between the mouth line and the gums and teeth may be noticed. When hooking this area don't try to include a lot of detail. Keep it simple so it doesn't become a visual distraction.

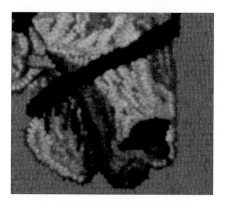

■ **HORSE'S MOUTH:** Usually, a dark line consisting of one or two rows of color will be seen. Try to duplicate this line paying particular attention to whether it's straight, curved, or wider in some areas than others. Choose a color and shade similar to what is seen in the visual.

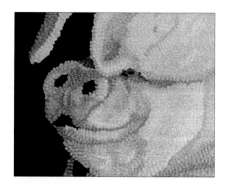

■ **PIG'S MOUTH:** The mouth line will be darker than the surrounding hair and may call for more than one row of hooking. Again, try to duplicate this line paying careful attention to the width and whether it's straight or curved. Sometimes I use a grayish-pink spot dye for the mouth line. This helps to keep it more natural looking. However, it can be much darker. This is one of those areas where it is good to experiment with several shades before the best choice is found. If the mouth is open be sure to duplicate the curve of the top line of the mouth.

■ COW'S MOUTH: The cow's mouth is darker than the surrounding hair and may call for more than one row of hooking. The shape of the mouth line will vary with the angle of the head and this will also affect the number of rows needed to duplicate what is seen on the visual. In a full-face pose the mouth will appear to run directly across the face curving slightly downward at each corner. In a side view the mouth will curve slightly upwards as it reaches the end of the mouth line.

■ MOUTH'S OF OTHER DOMESTIC ANIMALS: If the same basic format as the above mentioned animals is applied, you should be able to successfully hook any animal's mouth by using the visual as a guide.

## Teeth, Gums and Tongues

Once in a while you'll not only be confronted with tongues, but teeth and gums as well. I mention them now because in some situations the teeth will lie in front of the tongue. If this is the case, hook the teeth before the tongue.

(A good example of this can be seen in a side view or profile of the animal.)

If the gums are visible try to duplicate what is viewed on the visual without including any more detail than is absolutely necessary. Tone down any shades of red or pink used. If the gums are mottled in color (shades of red, pink, gray, and black) consider using spot dyes in the appropriate shades. This is another area that should not be emphasized.

> ## "Tongues are not attractive and should not become a focal point."

One of my least favorite things to hook is a tongue! But sometimes there it is, demanding to be hooked and not ignored. Here are some tips for hooking the tongue found in any type mouth. Start by making sure that it is the proper shape and not too large. Keep it as simple as possible and please, don't make the tongue too pink or too red! In photos and real life they may appear to be very bright, but trust me, this is the time to use a little artistic license and tone them down. Tongues are not attractive and should not become a focal point (If, once the head is completed, the eye is immediately drawn to the tongue, then it's become a focal point and needs to be reworked.)

First outline the tongue so it doesn't lose its shape and "grow" when it is hooked. Tongues are usually several shades and values giving them a slightly mottled appearance. This, of course, depends upon the size of the tongue. The smaller it is the less variation is seen. Spot dyes used alone or in conjunction with solid color (a swatch or wool off the bolt) work very well.

The back section of the tongue is usually the darkest portion because it appears as a shadow. Hook this portion first. Notice that there is often a darker section down through the center of the tongue. Complete this area using the shade chosen for the shadow or a shade lighter. Now proceed to fill the remaining portion of the tongue with a spot dye or a combination of spot dye and solid color. Make any necessary adjustments.

## Completing the Face

Once the eyes, nose, and mouth have been hooked, it is time to concentrate on the remainder of the face. To complete the face, add onto the finished portions one section at a time, until the entire head is completed.

### TIP: ANIMAL TEETH

Here are several guidelines to remember when hooking teeth. Keep them simple and not too large. Hook them in ivory or pale beige, not white. (The teeth will be distracting if hooked in white.) If the teeth are small and it's too difficult to hook each one, try eliminating a few and make the remaining teeth just a little larger.

# CHAPTER 4

# DOMESTIC CATS

**MISSY & ABBY,** *14 ³/₄" x 8", #3-cut wool on linen. Designed and hooked by Kathleen Donovan, Watchung, New Jersey, 2003.*

*These basic directions are for all domestic cats regardless of breed. If the cat has any distinct spots or color patterns, take a marker and outline them on the pattern.*

## Cat's Full Face

1 Start by checking the visual to see if the outline around the eye appears to continue out beyond the eye onto the face. On some cats this line will extend a short distance and on others it will continue out to or almost to the edge of the face and will generally call for more than one row of hooking. Try to duplicate this section paying close attention to direction, shape, width, and color. If this area appears to consist of several shades, try a spot dye.

2 Referring to the visual, notice that most cats have a smudge of color that adjoins the inner corner of the eye. Hook this small area in the appropriate color and length.

3 Directly under the eyes a distinct band of color may appear that begins next to or just below the smudge of color hooked in the corner of the eye. This band continues to the back edge of the eye. These rows of color can, on some cats, continue out onto the face. Use the visual, as a guide for how far out this band of color should continue.

4 The next area to address is the section that forms the bridge of the nose. This area is partially defined by hooking the nose and the smudges or dark areas at each inner corner of the eye. Now, hook a line, starting at the top and outer edge of the already completed nose and continue the line upwards until it

connects to the smudge or inner edge of the eye. (Repeat on the other side of the face.) Study the area between the two just hooked lines, and mark any sections that are formed by changes in color or shades of color. Hook these areas and then finish what remains. Most or all of this is worked in a vertical direction.

5 Now, turn your attention to the muzzle area. This area is outlined with a line that starts along each side of the bridge of the nose, rounds out and downward connecting to the outer edge of the mouth. The exact spot where this line begins can vary so study the visual carefully before drawing it on the pattern. To check the proportions take the visual and lay a strand of wool

on the outer edge of the muzzle and run it up to where it intersects the eye. This will show where the outer edge of the muzzle should be on the pattern. Hook the line on each side of the face.

The muzzle is where the whiskers are found. They grow out of a series of dots or bars of color. On small or medium-sized faces I usually eliminate a few of these dots so they don't occupy too much of the muzzle. Hook them to duplicate the color and shade seen on the visual. If whiskers are to be included, hook them now. Complete the remainder of the muzzle area in the correct shades and values of color in the direction hair appears to grow.

6 Next, observe the section directly below the band of color under the eye and above the muzzle. Depending on the breed of cat and its markings, this section can vary a great deal. It is impossible to address all of the variations, so these are some general guidelines for this area.

Remember the line or band of color hooked that continued out from the outer edge of each eye? Look at the visual and a line or shadow can probably be seen which adjoins the line and proceeds downward until it connects to the outline of the muzzle or chin. Hook the line or shadow as it appears on the visual, then finish the area from the nose over to this line or shadow. Work in the direction the hair appears to grow using the proper colors. (This is like the cheek of the cat.)

7 Hook the outline that forms the chin and then the area directly under the mouth line. This can be darker or lighter than the rest of the chin. Use the visual as a guide. Fill the remainder of the chin with appropriate color.

*Closeup of cat in* THE NANNY.

8 Hook the outline of the head between the ears. Look closely at the visual, and the line just hooked will continue out in front of the ears and to become the outline of the head. Hook the continuation of this line around both sides of the head as it appears on the visual.

9 Many cats have definite markings above the bridge of the nose and on the upper portion of the face. (This includes any bands of color above the eyes.) Hook all the bands of color and markings duplicating their angles and curves, just as they appear in the visual. Fill the rest of this area by hooking upward from the bridge of the nose. Most of the time the fur follows a vertical path up the center portion of the head and begins to gradually curve in front of the ears. By the time the area adjoining the eye is reached, the fur appears to grow out in a horizontal line. There will be some variation on each cat, so once again, study the visual and duplicate what is seen.

**Cat's Ears:** *Although ears can vary in size and shape from cat to cat, the same basic directions should be followed when hooking them.*

1 Hook the outline that forms the rim of the ear. (The rim can vary in width, being wider at the base of the ear and tapering towards the top of the ear). Duplicate the shape and width of the rim in the correct shades.

2 Go back to the completed line directly in front of the ear and hook in a vertical direction any hairs growing up from that line. (This fur or hair will enclose the bottom edge of the ear.)

3 Cats have guard hairs in their ears. These are tufts or sections of hair that grow out from the inner portion of the ear towards the outer edge of the ear. They vary in length and are very thick or solid where they attach to the inner ear. Hook the hairs in the direction they appear to grow. (When finished, they should not resemble teeth in a comb!) Don't hook these out beyond the outer rim of the ear, as they become a distraction to the eye.

4 After the guard hairs are hooked, finish the remainder of the inner ear. Hook this area to resemble what is seen in the visual, being sure to have enough contrast between each section of the ear to give an illusion of depth. If the ear has pink in it, use a pale shade so the cat doesn't look like it has an ear infection! Also, don't try to include too much detail in the ears. Keep them simple so that they don't become a focal point!

## Finishing the Head

Sometimes you will see another section of fur that starts in front or behind the ear and continues down along the side of the face. If this "ruff" is present, hook it now. (The length can vary according to the angle of the head, and in some cases, continue down under the cheeks to the chin.)

## Cat's Face Profile

1 Hook the outline of the head beginning between the ears and continuing down to the mouth line.

2 Follow steps 1 through 3; Cat's Full Face, page 22.

3 Follow portions of step 4 that apply; Cat's Full Face, page 22.

4 Follow steps 5 & 6; Cat's Full Face, pages 22 & 23.

*Closeup of cat in* THE NANNY.

5 Follow step 7; Cat's Full Face, page 23. Hook the chin back under the mouth line and back to the outline for the throat or body.

6 Finish the line or shadow in front of the ear closest to you. This line or shadow of color starts at the base of the ear, continues in front of the ear, and angles downward forming the back line of the face.

7 Refer to Cat's Ears, page 23, and the following:If the second ear located behind the outline of the face is turned so that the inner portion of the ear can't be seen, proceed using these directions.Hook the outline of the ear and any portion of the rim that's visible, then any visible highlights and shadows. Fill what remains. If the ear is turned so the inner ear and part of the back of the ear are seen, follow the Cat's Ears (page 23) section and then hook the back portion to the base of the ear.

8 Hook any portion of the face that remains above the eye up to the ear.

9 Complete any other unfinished area on the face.

LITTLE PRINCESS, 22" x 14", #3-cut wool on rug warp. Designed by Elizabeth Black. Hooked by Barbara Calvo, Whitehouse Station, New Jersey, 2003.

# CHAPTER 5

# DOGS

WINSTON, *15" x 15", #3-cut wool on rug warp. Designed by Elizabeth Black. Hooked by Sandra Brown, Pittsburgh, Pennsylvania, 1997.*

*The variations encountered on the faces of dogs are enormous! If the dog has any distinct spots or color patterns, take a marker and draw them on the pattern. The following are guidelines that apply to any face.*

## Dog's Full Face

1 Check the visual to see if the outline that encases the eye continues out beyond the eye onto the face. (It may extend a short distance or almost out to the edge of the face.) Hook this line to duplicate the length, width, angle, and color seen on the visual.

2 Study the area directly below the eye to determine the shape of this section. Does it appear to be rounded or triangular or does it resemble a bag or pouch under the eye? How far down onto the face does it go? Take a marker and outline this section on the pattern. By doing this a comparison can be made between what was marked and what is seen on the visual. If it isn't quite right, make the necessary changes before beginning to hook. Having this section the correct size and in the proper space is important because it helps to establish the width of the face between the eyes and above the nose. Once the shape is correct, hook this area in the colors selected paying special attention to the direction in which the hair grows.

3 Turn your attention to the area directly above the eyes and follow the same procedure used in completing the sections below the eyes. Again, correct placement is important.

HANK, *19" x 24", #3 and 4-cut wool on monk's cloth. Designed and hooked by Anna Boyer, Riverside, California, 2003.*

4 Continue by hooking the area just above the nose. It may consist of just a line or two of color that curves over the top of the nose and extends down the sides. Just above that area there may be a second section that is rounded or triangular in shape. In some dogs just one of the described sections may be apparent. There may be a definite difference in color between the two sections or a very subtle variation of color. Hook what is seen in the appropriate colors and shades.

5 If a definite line or shadow of color progresses up through the sections just above the nose, hook it as it appears. (This can be in addition to the sections just completed.) This line or shadow may continue almost all the way up the center of the head or serve as a "part" in the fur and not be very long. Finish any spots seen in this area or other definition lines.

6 Next, hook the outline of the head between the ears.

7 Complete the section between the eyes and the center portion of the forehead up to the outer line of the head. (Start above the finished sections of the nose and hook upward in a vertical direction.)

8 The next area to hook is the remaining portion of the forehead excluding the ears. This will be the area above each eye that hasn't been hooked (Notice how the hair begins to curve in an outward direction once it is beyond the center portion of the forehead.) Follow the same procedure we have used in other areas; hook in any definition lines first. This includes any lines that adjoin the ear or separate the ear from the rest of the head. Work in any pronounced highlights or shadows. While hooking, try to duplicate the "curved" direction of the hair.

9 Skip down to the area directly below the nose. Observe that on many dogs a vertical line is centered in the middle of the bottom line of the nose. This vertical line attaches to the center of the mouth line. Hook this line continuing outward on each side to form the mouth. On some dogs, the portion of the line that forms the mouth will vary in thickness and require more than a single row of hooking. Be careful to duplicate the curve of the mouth line as

POMERANIAN PILLOW, *14" x 16", #3-cut wool on rug warp. Designed and hooked by Elizabeth Black, Bentonville, Virginia, 1995.*

it establishes the shape of the lower portion of the face.

10 If a highlight or shadow is seen on each side of the vertical line, between the nose and the mouth, hook it now. (This can vary in width and can continue up along each side of the nose. Duplicate what is seen on the visual.)

11 Complete the remainder of the outline around the face.

12 The muzzle is the next area to hook. This is basically the area on each side of the nose down to the mouth line and outward including the cheeks and jowls. Begin by hooking any directional lines that divide the muzzle into sections to signify folds or wrinkles. Should small smudges of color or dots on the face appear where the whiskers would grow, hook them now. (I never put whiskers on dogs.) Fill the remaining area with the colors and shades seen on the visual. (Shadows and highlights first, then fill.) If this area is not as defined, it will still cover the lower portion of the face including the jowls.

13 Hook the section below the mouth line, which is the lower jaw and chin. This area will vary in size and shape depending on the breed of dog. If a tongue and/or teeth are present hook them now. (See section regarding tongues and teeth, page 21.) Hook the outline of the lower jaw and chin and then any highlights or shadows seen in this area. Fill the remaining area with the correct color.

**Dog's Ears** *Ears vary in structure and appearance depending on the breed. I will address the three most common types of ears.*

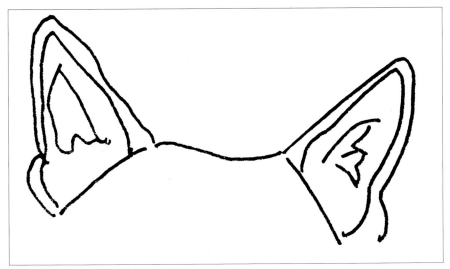

*Dog erect ear*

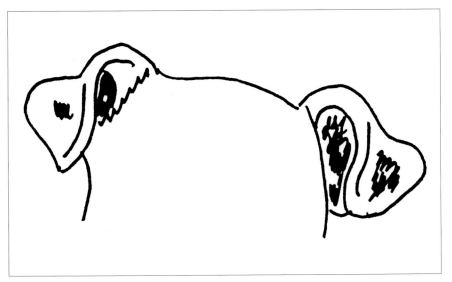

*Dog folded ear*

## The Erect Ear

Examples of this type are found on Chihuahuas, keeshounds, German shepherds and many other breeds.

1 Hook the outline and rim of the ear. The rim will vary in width and is usually wider at the base and tapering at the top. Finish the rim duplicating the colors and shades seen on the visual.

2 Go back to the line directly in front of the ear and hook, in a vertical direction any hair growing up from that line. (This will enclose the base of the ear.)

3 Just like cats, dogs have guard hairs in their ears. These are tufts or sections of hair that grow outward from the inner portion of the ear next to the rim, towards the outer edge of the ear. Hook them so they are solid where they attach to the ear but vary in length. (When finished hooking them, they shouldn't resemble teeth in a comb.)

4 Duplicate these hairs in the colors and the shades seen on the visual.

5 Hook the remainder of the inner ear to resemble what is seen on the visual, completing any dark spots or shadows first. If the ear contains pink coloration, use a pale shade so the dog doesn't look like it has two ear infections! To achieve an illusion of depth, make sure there is enough contrast between each part of the ear. Don't try to put too much detail in the ears. Keep them simple so they don't become a focal point.

## The Folded Ear

Examples of this type are found on Airedales, collies, bulldogs and many varieties of terriers.

1 Hook the V-shaped section that folds over the rest of the ear first. Do this by hooking the outline and any rim that is visible. Add the highlights and shadows. Fill the remaining part of the V-shape with the correct color.

2 The rest of the ear lies under this V-shape. Hook the remaining portion of the outline around the ear, then any tufts of hair growing up and out from the base of the ear. Next, complete any additional sections of hair growing out from the inner side of the ear where it attaches to the head. Hook any shadows or dark areas and fill the rest of the ear with the proper shades.

## The Long Ear

Examples can be seen on cocker spaniels, hounds, various toy breeds, and many others. It is also found on both longhaired and shorthaired dogs, and it is obvious that there is a very different look depending on the length of the hair.

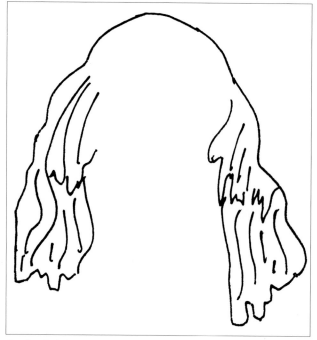

*Dog longhair long ear*

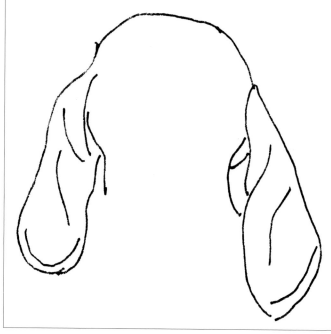

*Dog shorthair long ear*

## The Shorthaired Long Ear (front view)

1 Hook the outline taking care to duplicate the same shape that appears on the visual, then complete any lines that divide the ear into sections or appear as folds or wrinkles (Be sure they are properly curved or angled.)

2 Hook the section of the ear next to the head. This may appear as a folded section that continues down along the side of the face or it may look like a dark shadow. If it appears to be different than either of the examples mentioned, try to duplicate what is shown on the visual. Note: the first few rows should be dark enough to create a contrast between the head and the ear.

3 Proceed by hooking the next portion of the ear that adjoins the section just completed and continue in this manner until reaching the outer edge of the ear. (First work in any highlights or shadows that appear in the section being hooked and then fill.)

Remember to hook in the direction the hair grows. Referring back to the lines, angles, or curves finished earlier should help define each section of the ear.

## The Longhaired Long Ear

1 Complete the outline of the ear about halfway down on each side of the ear. These edges may appear to be undulating lines. Duplicate what is seen on the visual!

2 At first glance the ears can appear to be just a tangled mass of multi-length hair and color, but looking closely there is a pattern emerging. The hair varies in length and forms layers and sections. These will vary in shade and color. Using this premise, look at the visual and find the layer that starts at the top of the ear closest to the head. Remember length and color will help define the layer. Work this section in the direction the hair grows. If an undulating pattern is seen, that's what should be hooked. Continue hooking each layer in the same manner starting with the layer behind or just under the one just completed. Remember, always start with the top layer and work down through the various layers. Add more of an outline to the ear as needed.

3 The bottom edge of the ear may be uneven or ragged in appearance. I often modify this edge so it doesn't look too spiky when it is completed. After the ears on the dog's head have been hooked, the majority of the head and face will be finished. However, there may be a section beyond the eye, out to the edge of the head (or the ear if it's a long-eared dog) and downward, that hasn't been done. If this is the case, hook in any directional lines, then highlights and shadows, and fill in the remaining area with the correct colors and shades. Should there be any other areas not yet hooked, refer to the visual and finish them now.

BULLER, *15" x 15", #3- and 4-cut wool on rug warp. Designed and hooked by Mary Jean Whitelaw, Belle Meade, New Jersey, 2001.*

**Dog's Profile:** If the dog chosen for hooking has any distinct spots or color patterns, mark them on the pattern.

SAINT BERNARD DUMMY BOARD, *16" x 18", #3-cut wool on rug warp. Designed and hooked by Elizabeth Black, Bentonville, Virginia, 1997.*

1 Hook the outline of the face and head starting at the ears and continuing around the face to the neck. If the dog has a long ear, hook a holding line separating the ear from the face.

2 Follow step 1 for Dog's Full Face, page 25.

3 Study the area directly below the eye to determine the shape and angle of this section. Directional lines, highlights and shadows, or a combination of the three may define this area. Mark this section on the pattern then hook it in the correct colors and values, beginning with any definition lines, highlights, and/or shadows. Pay attention to the direction the hair grows and hook in the same direction.

4 Hook the area directly above the eye and behind the eye following the same procedure used for the area below the eye (step 1; Dog's Full Face, page 25).

5 Refer to step 4; Dog's Full Face, page 26. (Exception: On some dogs this area may appear to be one solid color. Hook it using the procedure that best fits the dog.)

6 Hook the muzzle. This section, starting at the outline of face, includes the portion above the nose up to the hooked section under the eye and down to the mouth line. This also includes any area behind the mouth line including the jaw and jowl. Refer to step 13 for guidance in hooking this area.

7 Complete any remaining area above the nose to the top of the head.

8 Finish any other area above and behind the eye to the top of the head or to the ear.

9 Read the section on Dog's Ears (pages 27 & 28) and choose the example that best suits the dog, then hook as instructed.

# CHAPTER 6

# HORSES

*JAZZ, 22" x 23", #3-cut wool on rug warp. Designed and hooked by Carol Murphy, Hopkinton, New Hampshire, 1995.*

*Although there are numerous types of horses and other species
in the horse family, you can basically use the same directions
for any that you may encounter.*

## Horse's Full Face

1 Hook the eyes. (Refer to chapter on Faces; Eyes, pages 15 & 16.)

2 Follow directions given in steps 2 and 3; Horse Profile, page 31.

3 Next hook the nostrils. (Refer to chapter on Faces; Noses, page 18.)

4 Hook the mouth line, which in this case is the bottom line of the muzzle.

5 Complete the outline around the head duplicating the color and the shape.

6 Turn your attention to the section known as the muzzle. (The muzzle is the portion of the head that includes the areas above and below the nostrils and the mouth.) At the upper edge of the muzzle is a slightly curved line that

separates it from the rest of the face. This line can continue downward to become part of the outline of the muzzle. Hook this line, duplicating it as it appears on your visual.

7 Hook the muzzle area. (Refer to step 7; Horse Profile, page 31.)

8 Hook the chin duplicating the colors and shades seen on the visual.

*Horse profile*

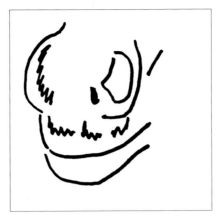

*Horse muzzle*

9 Complete the forelock. (Refer to step 9; Horse Profile, page 32.)

10 If the horse's face is spotted or contains a blaze, refer to step 10; Horse Profile, page 32.

11 Work in any other definition lines or shadows that break the face down into sections.

12 Finish the remaining areas on the face with the appropriate colors or values.

13 Hook the ears, which appear to sit just behind the outline of the head. Complete the outline of the ear just as it appears on the visual then any rim seen on the ear filling it in with the proper shades of color. (The rim can be most of the ear in this pose.) Notice a shadow that adjoins the rim and defines the inner portion of the ear. Finish this shadow and then the inner portion of the ear, always trying to hook in the direction the hair grows. Any small section remaining at the outer base of the ear where the ear connects to the head should be worked now.

14 If the mane is visible on either side of the head, hook the outline of the neck and then the portion of the mane that is visible. (Work in the highlights, shadows and fill.) Hook the hair in the mane in the direction it appears to grow.

15 Complete any portion of the body, chest, or neck visible around or behind the head. (Definition is first, then highlights and shadows. Fill what remains.)

## Horse's Profile

1 Hook the eyes. (Refer to chapter on Faces; Eyes, page 15 & 16.)

2 Work any definition lines that form a pocket under the eye and a lid above the eye. Add any other lines or shadows that immediately adjoin the eye.

3 Fill the lid and pocket area with the appropriate shades of color. (Be sure to hook in the direction the hair appears to grow.)

4 Next, hook the nostrils. (Refer to chapter on Faces; Horse's Noses, page 18.)

5 Complete the mouth line. (Refer to chapter on Faces; Horse's Mouths, page 20.)

6 Hook the outline around the head duplicating both the color and shape. The bone structure of the face helps to define various parts of the face. The cheek area is clearly defined by the rounded and curved line that is an extension of the outline of the head. Notice how this curved line continues on into the face. Hook the continuation of this line now. If a subtle rounded and curved line running across the top of the muzzle is seen, and it curves downward to the lower jaw line, hook this line now. (Reminder: The muzzle is part of the head that includes the area above the nostrils, the upper and lower lip, and the chin.)

*"The bone structure of the face*
*helps to define various parts of the face."*

Also notice a horizontal line that runs from the edge of the muzzle, just above and back of the mouth line that connects to the line that forms the cheek. Complete this line now. This line is horizontal to the outer edge of the face.

7 Continue by hooking the muzzle area. The color will vary and often consists of several subtly blended shades. If there is a pink tone to part of the muzzle, be very careful that too bright a shade isn't used. The muzzle is a good area to use a spot-dye to achieve that mottled look. As usual, hook in the direction the hair appears to grow.

8 The next segment to add is the ears. Start by checking the drawing to be sure the ears are the correct size and shape. Even though the horse is in pro-

file both ears are probably visible. Hook the outline of the nearest ear, taking care to use the proper shades to duplicate any highlights or dark areas. (If a portion of the outline resembles a rim, treat it as such.) Any dark shadows seen at the base of the ear where it joins the head should be hooked next, then any other highlights seen on the surface of the ear. Complete the remainder of the ear, taking care to blend the various shades. Work the other ear applying the same basic steps. If a portion of the inner ear is visible refer to step 13; Horse Full Face, page 31.

9 Next, turn your attention to the forelock. This is the portion of the mane that lies between the ears and partially covers the forehead. Hook in any dark lines that divide the hair into sections or layers, then any highlights or shadows and fill what remains. This will be hooked in an upward direction.

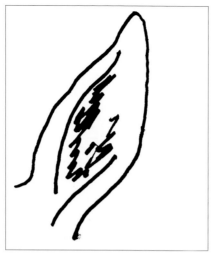

*Horse ear*

11 Look to see if there is a line or shadow of color that starts at the back of the eye. It will vary in the angle or curve it follows as well as the length and width. Hook this line or shadow in the appropriate color and values.

12 Study the face and complete any other definition lines or shadows that break the face down into sections.

the head beginning between the ears to form the top outline of the rest of the head and the neck. The mane grows off of this line. When hooking the mane, duplicate the direction it follows. Work in any directional lines, highlights, and shadows and then fill what remains.

15 Next, the bottom outline of the head or neck should be hooked, then whatever is left of the head or neck below the mane.

**Horse's ³/₄ Angle:** *For the head that is slightly turned follow the directions for the horse in profile. The major differences are the second eye and nostril may be visible. Hook them when the other eye and nostril are hooked. Complete all of the face and head, and then finish whatever sections remain above and below the smaller, or second eye.*

*"The muzzle is part of the head that includes the area above the nostrils, the upper and lower lip, and the chin."*

10 There are various patterns of color that can appear on the face. One of the most common is the blaze. This is a section that runs vertically, from the forehead down the middle of the face. It varies in length, size, and width. If the horse has this type of marking, outline it on the pattern and hook it in a vertical direction. Should the horse have other markings on its face, mark them on the pattern and complete these sections of color before hooking the surrounding area.

13 Finish the remaining areas on the face with the appropriate colors and values in the following sequence: the area in front and above the eye, along the forelock and up to the base of the ear, the cheek area, the portion under the eye down to the muzzle and out to the edge of the head, and the remaining section between the cheek and below the muzzle.

14 The area above the cheek is part of the head that eventually becomes the neck. Hook the outline of

# CHAPTER 7

# PIGS

**PIGTORIAL**, *40" x 30", #3-cut wool on rug warp. Designed and hooked by Elizabeth Black, Bentonville, Virginia, 1999.*

*For me, the biggest challenge in hooking a pig is finding a suitable combination of colors. When correctly placed, the subtle changes of color and values create the highlights and shadows that give a pig its form and dimension. After deciding on my basic colors, I look for spot dyes that will meet my needs, including some solid colors for distinct definition lines.*

## Pig's Profile

1  Hook the eye if visible. (Refer to the chapter on Faces; Eyes, page 15 & 16.) If the ear covers the eye hook the outline of the entire ear.

2  Hook any definition lines that form a pocket under the eye and a lid above the eye. Add any other lines that adjoin the eye.

3  Fill the lid and pocket area with the appropriate shades of color. (Try to work in the direction the hair appears to grow.)

4  Hook the nostril and the snout. (Refer to section on Pig's Nose and Snout, page 18.)

5  Complete the mouth line. (Refer to section on Pig's Mouth, page 20.)

6  Hook the outline of the face beginning just above the snout and continuing up between the ears to the forehead.

7  Hook any wrinkles or definition lines seen above the snout. (Complete one row and at least a partial row to keep them from looking like strings of

color.) If the pig's head is small, reduce the number of wrinkles so it retains some definition.

8  Finish the bottom outer line of the head from the mouth back, including the section that forms the chin, jowl, and neck.

9  Look for a line that begins a short distance beyond the eye and continues downward. A break may appear in this line, and then it will begin again, and continue to the lower outline of the head. Hook this line as it appears.

10 At the back edge of the mouth line a highlight or shadow may be seen that forms a curved band of color continuing down to the outline of the head. This band of color defines the chin and the area back to the definition line hooked in step 9. Complete this band of color.

11 Hook the chin area, working in the direction the hair appears to grow. First duplicate any highlights or shadows then fill the area that remains.

12 Finish the area above the snout and mouth approximately up to the inner corner of the eye. Study the direction the hair grows and the color patterns in this area. Hook the shadows and highlights first, then fill with the appropriate color.

13 Complete the area from behind the eye to the line hooked in step 9. Continue by working the remainder of this section down to the bottom outline of the head. (This section includes the cheek and jowl.) Again, hook any highlights and shadows first, then fill, always hooking in the direction the hair grows.

14 Hook the ears next. In profile both ears will probably be seen. The closest ear may be different in shape and the inner ear may be exposed. Finish the entire outline of this ear. If a rim is visible, complete it now. Hook any tufts of hair growing in the ear and adjoining the rim. Any dark shadows within the inner section of the ear should be finished next, then fill whatever area is left within the ear in the appropriate colors and values. If a portion of the ear is visible at the base of the ear, under the rim, complete it now. Should this ear loop down over the eye, proceed in the following manner. Since the

entire ear was outlined earlier, now add any lines that define a rim or break the ear up into sections, then hook the highlights and shadows and fill.

The other ear lies behind the outline of the head. First, hook the outline of this ear. Should a rim or partial rim be visible, it should be done now. Complete any highlights or shadows seen and then fill the remaining portion. If some of the inside of the ear is visible on either ear, hook it now. In the event

**PIG SHAPED PILLOW,** *16" x 16", #3-cut wool on rug warp. Designed and hooked by Elizabeth Black, Bentonville, Virginia, 1990.*

*Pig folded ear*

that the second ear also flops over, it should be worked in the same way previously outlined.

15 Hook the remainder of the face, in front of the eye, up to the top of the head.

16 Finish any remaining area of the face located in front of the definition line hooked in step 9.

17 Near or just above the base of the closest ear another definite line will curve slightly back and down-

ward ending just in front of the front leg. A portion of this line can be seen, even if only the face and head are being completed. Hook this line and the entire area starting behind the line done in step 9 up to this line. Make sure to hook the hair in the direction it appears to grow.

18 Any remaining areas between the ears and behind the ears should be finished at this time.

**Pig's ³/₄ Angle:** *For the head that is slightly turned that shows ³/₄ of the face, follow the directions for the Pig's Profile, page 33. The major differences are that the other eye and nostril may be partially visible. Hook them when the other eye and nostril are finished. After completing all of the rest of the head, hook whatever remains above and below the smaller eye. (This will usually appear to be a smaller section.)*

## Full Face Ears Over Eyes

1. Follow step 1; Pig's Profile, page 33. If the eyes are covered or partially covered by the ears, outline the ears and then hook the visible portion of the eyes.

2. Follow steps 2 through 4, when applicable, of Pig's Profile, page 33.

3. Hook the mouth line. Refer to section on Pig's Mouth, page 20. If the mouth is open, complete the area inside the mouth to duplicate what is seen on the visual.

4. Finish the ears next. (The outline was previously hooked.) Next do any visible rim then any creases, folds, or definition lines that are present and any highlights or shadows. Fill the remainder of the ears with the appropriate shades and values.

5. Complete the area directly above the snout. Start by hooking any def-

*Close up of pig in PIGTORIAL*

inition lines, creases, or wrinkles that are present. If a triangular or rounded area of color just above the snout is seen, do it now.

6. Continue moving upward between the eyes and the ears to about even with the top of the ear. Most or all of this section is worked in a vertical direction. Use the visual for guidance.

7. Hook the outline across the top of the head.

8. Finish the forehead area duplicating the direction the hair grows.

9. Hook the outline around the remainder of the head.

10. Complete the chin's highlights and shadows, then fill.

11. One or two more definition lines that divide the face into sections may be seen. One begins just beyond the outer corners of the eyes and curves down connecting to the outer line of the head. The second line begins behind the ears and curves down to connect to the outer line of the head. Hook these lines and any others

*"After completing all of the rest of the head, hook whatever remains above and below the smaller eye."*

*Close up of pigs in* PIGTORIAL

that may divide the face into sections. Each section should be completed beginning with those closest to the snout.

12 Finish any remaining areas on the face.

## Erect Ears

1 Refer to steps 1 through 4; Pig's Profile, page 33. (Two eyes will be hooked instead of one.)

2 Refer to step 3; Pig's Full Face, page 35.

3 Refer to step 5; Pig's Full Face, page 35.

4 Continue hooking upward between the eyes to the top of the eyes. Most or all of this section is worked vertically. Use the visual for guidance.

5 Hook the outline across the top of the head between the ears. Continue this line as it curves in front of the ears and downward becoming the outline of the face and head.

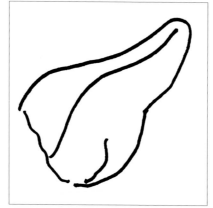

*Pigs erect ear*

6 Next the forehead and the remainder of the upper portion of the face. (This includes the area to the top of the head and the area above the eyes to the outline in front of the ears. Continue by hooking the area on each side of the eye that extends to the outline of the face.)

7 Hook the ears, the outline, and then the rim of the ear. (The rim may widen on one side and become the base portion of the ear.) Fill the rim with the correct shades and values and complete any dark areas or shadows seen inside the ear.

Complete the outline on the top portion of the ear and finish any rim you see. Fill the rim with the appropriate shades and values. Hook any highlights and shadows and then fill the remaining area. Finish the outline on the portion of the ear that is behind the section of the ear just completed. Do the highlights and shadows and fill.

8 The definition lines that outline the cheeks should be finished next, followed by any additional lines on the cheeks such as creases or wrinkles. Hook any highlights or shadows that appear on the cheeks and fill what remains with the appropriate colors and values.

9 Hook the outline of the chin following the same procedure used in step 8 (Pig's Profile, page 33).

10 Finish the section of the face that adjoins the outer edge of the cheeks. This section usually covers all the area from the eyes out to the edge of the face. (Depending on the pose, it can continue down around and under the chin.) Follow the same procedure that applies from step 8. Pay close attention to the direction the hair grows. Use the visual as a guide.

11 If there are more areas on the pig's head that need to be hooked continue in the same manner described in steps 8 and 10.

# CHAPTER 8

# COWS

*Close up of cow from* PEACEABLE KINGDOM

*Holy cow! Do you have any idea how many breeds of cattle have existed? For the sake of space and my sanity I'm giving the basic directions for hooking a cow's face. Pay attention to the visual and add whatever is needed to individualize the face.*

## Cow's Face Profile

1 Hook the eyes (Refer to the chapter on Faces; Eyes, pages 15 & 16.)

2 Next complete any definition lines that form a lid above the eye or a pouch under the eye.

3 If a pronounced color pattern or spot is visible around the eye, mark the outline with a marker and hook the outline in the correct color.

4 Fill all the areas in steps 2 and 3 with the appropriate shades and values of color.

5 Hook the nostril. (Refer to chapter on Faces; Noses, page 19.)

6 Next hook the mouth line. (Refer to chapter on Faces; Mouths, page 21.)

7 Finish the outline of the head, beginning at the top of the head and continuing around the face, including the neck.

8 Complete any definition lines that define specific areas such as the cheeks, nose area, lower jaw, and sections of the neck. These lines can also define creases and wrinkles.

9 Hook the area around the nostril that forms the nose or muzzle. Begin by working the outline around this sec-

tion, then any highlights or shadows, and fill whatever remains. Spot dyes will give a subtle change of color that is often needed.

10 Turn your attention to the ear and horns if visible. Should the horn partially cover the ear, hook the horn first. If the second horn is partially visible beyond the head, hook it after completing the head. (Refer to the section on Antlers and Horns, page 45.)

■ COW'S EAR (WITH INNER SECTION VISIBLE): Complete the outline of the ear and any rim that is visible. (The rim may vary in width.) Hook any tufts of

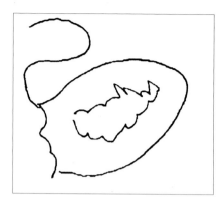

*Cow ear front view*

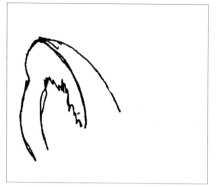

*Cow ear back portion*

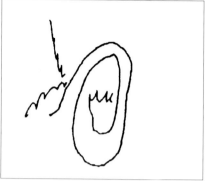

*Cow ear angled*

hair growing inside the ear out from the rim. (These will be irregular in length.) Hook any highlights and shadows seen within the ear. Fill the remainder of the inner ear and be sure there is enough contrast between the various sections of the ear so it doesn't lose definition.

■ COW'S EAR (SHOWING BACK PORTION): Hook the outline of the ear then any visible rim and the highlights and shadows as they appear. The remainder of the ear should be completed in the appropriate shades and values. Remember to work in the direction the hair appears to grow.

11 If the cow is spotted or has areas of contrasting color, take a marker and outline these areas now.

12 Hook the portion of the face above the nose that proceeds to the top of the head.

13 Finish the remaining area above the eye up to the top of the head.

14 Now work the area that adjoins the nose and forms the cheek.

15 Complete any remaining portion that is above the cheek and under the eye.

16 Hook whatever area remains on the lower portion of the face. (This will be the chin and any other sec-

tion below the cheek back to the ear.)

17 Should a portion of the neck be visible, finish it now. (Hook any definition lines, add highlights and shadows, and fill.)

## Cow's Full Face

1 Follow the steps 1 through 4; Cow Profile, page 37.

2 Hook the nostrils. (Refer to the chapter on Faces; Cow's Noses, page 19.)

3 Hook the mouth line (Refer to chapter on Faces; Cow's Mouths, page 21.)

4 Follow step 9; Cow's Profile, page 37.

5 Hook the outline of the head between the ears or horns.

6 Complete the remainder of the outline around the face to the mouth.

7 Finish the outline around the chin, adding any lines, creases or wrinkles that are visible in this area. Hook in the highlights and shadows and fill the remaining area of the chin.

8 If there appears to be a separate section above the forehead and up to the outline of the head, do this section now. On some cattle the horns extend

*Close up of cows from* INSIDE THE ARK

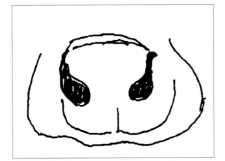

*Cow muzzle front view*

from the section above the forehead and on others the horns are just below it. Usually a subtle distinction can be seen between this area and the top of the forehead. Complete this area as it appears on the visual.

9 Hook the center portion of the face starting just above the nose and continuing upwards between the eyes to the top of the head or to the section completed in step 8. This area may be defined by lines or shadows on each side of it. If so, hook a line, in the appropriate shade, on each side to separate it from the remainder of the face. Hook any wrinkles, creases, or definition lines seen in this section, then the highlights and shadows and fill what remains. Most or all of this will be worked vertically.

10 The remaining portions of the face and head above the eyes should be finished next. Hook any definition lines, creases or wrinkles first, then the highlights and shadows and fill what remains.

11 Complete the area on each side of the eyes outward to the edge of the head.

12 Do the remainder of the face starting with any definition lines, creases, or wrinkles that are visible. Continue by hooking the highlights and

shadows then fill what remains.

13 If other areas are visible beyond or under the head that you wish to include, hook them now. Proceed by doing the outline, definition lines, creases, wrinkles, highlights and shadows, and then fill what remains.

14 Refer to step 10; Cow's Profile, page 37.

**Cow's ³/₄ Angle:** *For the head that is slightly turned and shows ³/₄ of the face follow the directions for the Cow's Full Face, page 37.*

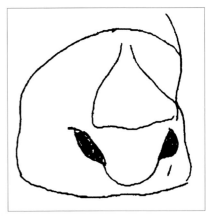

*Cow muzzle ³/₄ view*

*"On some cattle the horns extend from the section above the forehead and on others the horns are just below it."*

*Close up of cow from* **PEACEABLE KINGDOM**

39

# CHAPTER 9

# WILD ANIMALS

**TIGRIS**, *43" x 22 ¹/₂", #3-cut wool on monk's cloth. Designed and hooked by Ann Winterling, Concord, New Hampshire, 1990.*

*There is a growing interest in hooking members of the wild kingdom. I can't begin to discuss every animal, so I've chosen some of the more popular ones and grouped those that are related or have similar characteristics together.*

## The Big Cats' Faces—Lions, Tigers, Leopards and Cheetahs

All cats, from the pampered pet to the king of the jungle, share the same basic structure. Because of this similarity the same steps can be followed to hook a wild cat's face as were used for a domestic cat. If the cat chosen to be hooked is spotted, striped, or has a color pattern composed of obvious changes of color, mark these areas on the pattern. You may choose to eliminate a few stripes or spots, if the cat on the pattern is small. (On spotted cats I often reduce the number of spots and slightly enlarge some of those that remain.)

■ WILD ANIMAL'S EYES: The shape is important, so be sure the outline of the

**TIGER PILLOW,**
*18" x 20", #3-cut wool on rug warp. Designed and hooked by Elizabeth Black, Bentonville, Virginia, 1993.*

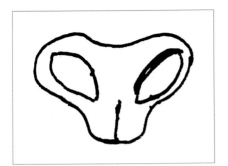
*Cheetah nose*

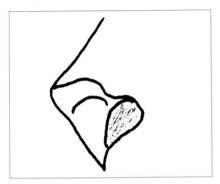
*Cheetah nose side view*

*Cheetah ear*

Duplicate the outline of the mouth and the color of the lips. If teeth are present hook them next and then any portion of the tongue that is visible. Hook the mouth. (Refer to section on cat's mouth, also teeth, gums, and tongue.)

**JAGUAR PILLOW,** *20" x 20", #3-cut wool on rug warp. Designed and hooked by Elizabeth Black, Bentonville, Virginia, 1993.*

eye duplicates the outline seen on the visual. Sometimes the top portion of the outline cuts off the upper portion of the eye. All the big cats have circular eyes. Hook the eyes. (Refer to section on Eyes, pages 15 & 16.)

**WILD ANIMAL'S NOSE:** A wild cat's nose is very similar to that of a domestic cat only larger. On some cats, such as a tiger, there is a pink or salmon tone to a portion of their nose. Choose the shade used very carefully so the nose doesn't become a bright focal point. (I prefer to use a spot dye for this area.) Hook the nose. (Refer to the section on Cat's Nose, page 17.)

**WILD ANIMAL'S MOUTH:** When the mouth is closed it resembles that of a house cat and only a shadow for the mouth line may be seen. If the mouth is open the lips will be seen, and they can be black, flesh colored, or mottled depending on the cat.

## Big Cats' Full Face (Except Male Lions)

1 Follow steps 1 through 3; Cat's Full Face, page 22.

2 Follow step 4; Cat's Full Face, page 22. Pay attention to the shape of the outline, as it will vary from one breed to another.

3 Follow step 5; Cat's Full Face, pages 22 & 23.

4 Follow step 6; Cat's Full Face, page 23. Hook any stripes or spots in this section before the rest of the section is filled.

5 Follow step 7; Cat's Full Face, page 23. The outline of the chin may appear to be irregular to reflect the variation in the length of the hair.

6 Follow steps 8 and 9; Cat's Full Face, page 23.

7 The position of the ear will vary depending on the breed of cat. For the ear that is primarily rim and inner ear, follow the section on Cat's Ears as described in Cat's Full Face, page 23. If the ear shows a large amount of the outside or back of the ear, hook this first. Continue by hooking any definite markings, highlights or shadows that you see. Finish what remains on this part of the ear and the remainder of the outline around the rest of the ear. Complete any rim that is visible on this portion of the ear and any hairs seen within the ear; fill what remains.

8 Follow section on Finishing the Head as described in Cat's Full Face, pages 23 & 24.

## Male Lion Full Face

1 Follow instructions for steps 1 through 7; Big Cats' Full Face, pages 22 & 23.

2 Hook any outline at the top of the head that isn't covered by the mane and the remainder of the outline around the face.

3 All adult male lions have manes and even "teenage" males have a suggestion of what's to come. The mane lies behind the ears and on either side of the cheeks covering or partially covering the

*LION PILLOW, 20" x 20", #3-cut wool on rug warp. Designed and hooked by Elizabeth Black, Bentonville, Virginia, 1993.*

neck and the shoulders. However, sometimes depending on the angle of the head, the mane can partially cover one ear or both. In this case hook the portion of the mane covering the ear before the ear is hooked. Then hook whatever portion of the ear that's visible. Continue with the rest of the mane. If the mane doesn't cover the ears, follow step 7; Big Cats' Full Face, page 41, and then hook the mane.

Look carefully at the visual and try to see the multiple sections or layers of hair that form the mane. Some of the things that help define these various areas are highlights, shadows, and sections of hair that are similar in length or appear as separate tufts. The direction the hair follows will also help to divide the mane into sections and layers. I find it helpful to mark these sections before beginning to hook the mane. Hook the mane section by section starting with the portion that forms the top layer, then the section that adjoins what was just completed directly under it. Continue in this manner, section by section, layer by layer.

4. Follow step 9; Cat's Full Face, page 23.

5. Follow instructions for Finishing the Head; Cat's Full Face, page 24.

## Big Cat's Face—Profile (Except Male Lions)

1. Follow step 1; Cat's Face Profile, page 24.

2. Follow steps 1 through 3; Cat's Full Face, page 22.

3. Follow portions of step 4; Cat's Full Face, page 22. (This may appear as a broken line or more as a shadow.)

4. Follow steps 5 and 6; Cat's Full Face, pages 22 & 23.

5. Follow step 7; Cat's Full Face, page 23. Hook all of the chin section under the mouth line and back to the outline for the throat and body.

6. Follow step 6; Cat's Profile, page 24, and step 7; Big Cats' Full Face, page 41. (Use whatever applies.)

7. Follow step 9; Cat's Full Face, page 23.

8. Follow step 1; Cat's Full Face, page 22.

## Male Lion Face in Profile

1. Hook the entire outline around the head visible from the mane down to the mouth line.

2. Follow steps 1 through 3; Cat's Full Face, page 22.

3. Follow portions of step 4 that apply from Cat's Full Face, page 22. The line discussed in this step may appear to be more of a shadow than a line or it may be a broken line.

4. Follow steps 5 and 6; Cat Full Face, pages 22 & 23.

5. Follow step 7; Cat Full Face, page 23. Hook the entire chin back under the mouth line and back to the outline for the throat and body.

6. Complete any portion of the rim visible on the closest ear. Any hairs or tufts of hair growing out from the rim should be hooked next, and if there is another tuft of hair at the base of the rim or ear, finish it now. Hook any section seen in front of the rim that creates a shadow. Outline the rest of the ear (this will be the back of the ear) and fill with the appropriate shades and values. The remaining ear if visible, will be finished after the mane is hooked. Duplicate what is seen in the visual.

*Close up from* TIGERS IN PARADISE

THE CAMP, 55" x 40", #3-cut wool on linen. Designed and hooked by Cynthia Sweeney, Fairfield, Connecticut, 2000. Photograph courtesy of Cynthia Sweeney.

## Animal Faces with Antlers (Deer, Elk, and Moose):

*The same basic directions apply in hooking the faces of the animals mentioned as well as other antlered species.*

### Full Face

1 Hook the eyes. Refer to the section on Eyes, pages 15 & 16.

2 DEER & ELK NOSE: First hook the outline of the nose, the nostrils, and then the center portion of the nose around the nostrils and any highlights and shadows that are visible. Finish what remains using the proper shades and values. MOOSE NOSE: Hook the nostrils if visible. (Notice how they are close to the edge of the muzzle.) Finish any rim of color seen around the nostrils,

then any highlights and shadows adjacent to the nostrils.

3 Hook the mouth line. (It may appear to be the bottom line of the muzzle.)

4 Complete the outline of the muzzle on each side of the face. These lines will extend upwards from the mouth line to above the nostrils. (Duplicate the shape seen on the visual.) The remaining area of the muzzle starting with any visible lines, highlights, or shadows should be hooked next, then fill whatever remains.

5 Hook the outline of the chin and any visible spots, highlights, or shadows. Fill what remains using the proper shades and values, working in the direction the hair appears to grow.

6 Refer to steps 2 through 5; Dog's Full Face, pages 25 & 26. (Yes, this is a very different creature but the same directions and sequence apply so just ignore the word "dog" and proceed!)

7 DEER & ELK—BUCKS & BULLS: Hook the outline of the head visible between the antlers and between the antlers and the ears. For the Bull Moose, hook the outline of the head between the ears. DOES AND COWS (ALL SPECIES): Hook the outline of the head between the ears

*Moose front profile*

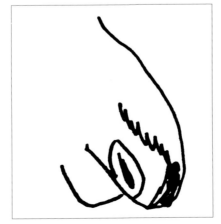

*Moose muzzle profile*

*Moose muzzle ³/₄ view*

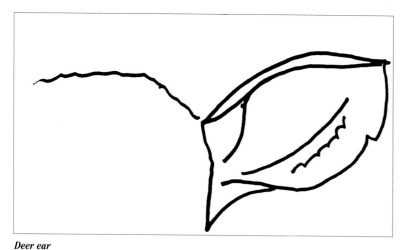

*Deer ear*

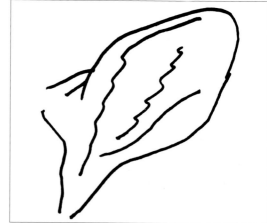

*Elk ear*

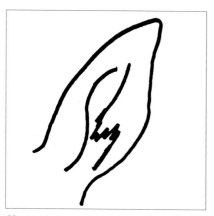

*Moose ear*

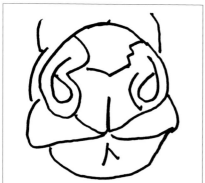

*Deer nose profile*

*Deer nose frontal*

*Elk nose frontal*

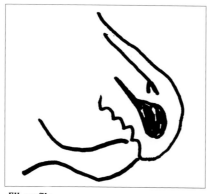

*Elk profile*

and continue the line down in front of the ears to the muzzle. At this point study the visual carefully and proceed using the directions for the animal. **BULL ELK:** Notice the definition line that runs outward from each antler and continues down around the outer edge of the eye. This line continues and becomes the outer edge of the face down to the edge of the muzzle. Hook the entire line as it appears on each side of the face. Look for a curved line that forms either a highlight or shadow in front of the antlers. Hook this line in the appropriate color. Several areas at the top of the face and head have now been defined. **BULL MOOSE AND BUCK:** There is a definition line that runs between the antlers and connects to the outer line of the antlers. The line continues in front of the antlers and down along the side of the face to the muzzle. Hook the entire line in the appropriate color.

8 **ALL SPECIES—MALE AND FEMALE:** Start at the completed muzzle area and hook upward between the eyes to any definition line separating the forehead into sections. (If this line isn't visible continue hooking to the top of the head.)

9 Refer to step 8; Dog's Full Face, page 26.

10 Hook the antlers and the ears. If the antlers cover or partially cover the ears, do the antlers first then the ears. **ANTLERS:** Hook the outline of the antlers and any hair growing upwards from the base of the antlers. Antlers may appear to consist of various individual sections. View these sections as layers and hook those that

*Close up from* INSIDE THE ARK

behind the ears or antlers.

2 Hook the eye. Refer to section on Eyes, pages 15 & 16.

3 Hook the nose. Refer to step 2; Antlered Animals' Full Face, page 43.

4 Refer to steps 2, 3, & 5; Horse's Profile, page 31.

5 Read steps 6 & 7; Horse's Profile, page 31, and apply what is relevant to the animal.

6 If you are hooking a female, complete the ear at this time. Refer to Antlers and Ears, Full Face, page 43, and the following additional information: The second ear, if visible, may only show the back of the ear. After the outline of the second ear is hooked, add any highlights and shadows and fill what remains. Use the visual as a guide.

If you are hooking a male and the antlers cover or partially cover the ears, hook the antlers first and then the ears. (Refer to sections regarding

> *"Antlers may appear to consist of various individual sections. View these sections as layers and hook those that aren't covered by other portions of the antlers first."*

aren't covered by other portions of the antlers first. Proceed by completing the layer that lies behind the portion just finished. Continue in this manner until the antlers are finished. As you begin each section, hook in any directional lines, highlights, and shadows first. Fill what remains with the appropriate shades and values. EARS—ALL SPECIES MALE AND FEMALE: Hook the outline of the ear and any rim on the ear that is visible, then any hairs growing from the rim towards the inner portion of the ear and whatever portion of the inner ear that's visible. If there is a section of the ear between the head and the rim of the ear that needs to be hooked, do so now using the visual for guidance.

11 To hook any portion of the face or head that remains, start by

adding lines that divide the face or head into sections and then hook any highlights or shadows that are visible. Fill what remains.

## Antlered Animals in Profile (All Species Male and Female)

1 Starting between the ears, hook any visible portion of the outline of the head including the neck. Complete any of the outline of the head visible

Antlers and Ears Full Face, page 43. See additional information about the second ear in the first paragraph of step 6.)

7 All species male and female. Refer to steps 1 through 13; Horse's Profile, page 31. Read these steps and apply what is relevant to your animal.

8 Hook any areas that remain on the face.

*PANDA, 18 ¹/₂" x 19 ³/₄", #2, 3, and 4-cut wool on rug warp. Designed by Elizabeth Black. Hooked by Jean Harris Coon, Newport Beach, California, 2001.*

*Bear nose front view*

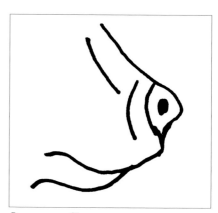

*Bear nose profile*

## Bears—(All species plus the Giant Panda)

**FACES:** All bears share similar physical characteristics, so use the following directions for all species and the Giant Panda. Bears are predominantly one color—black, some shade of brown, or white. (Of course the panda will be black and white.)

## Bear Full Face

1 Hook the eyes and nose. The size and shape of a bear's nose can vary from breed to breed. The outline of the nose and the nostrils should be hooked first, then the line that begins at the center of the base of the nose and continues upward. (This line varies in length and can end below or between the nostrils. Check the visual.) Hook any highlights or shadows and whatever remains. (Refer to sections on Eyes, pages 15 & 16, and Nose, page 17.)

2 If the outline around the eye extends outward from the back of the eye onto the face, hook the continuation of this line. (It may appear as a line or shadow.) Complete this area to duplicate what is seen on the visual.

3 Focus on the areas immediately under the eyes and the inner corner of each eye. This may look like a shadow or appear as a definite shape such as a bag or pouch. Mark the shape on the pattern in the proper colors and shades hooking in the direction the hair grows.

4 Repeat the process in step 3 in the areas directly above the eyes.

5 Concentrate on the area directly above the nose. Look closely at the visual and a line will be noticed that begins near the top outer edge of the nose, on each side of the nose, and continues upward to the inner corner of each eye. These two lines define the bridge of the nose. Hook them in the correct color along with any definite shapes or patterns of color seen between these two lines. Continue by adding any highlights, lines, or shadows seen in this same area and fill what remains. This section will end between the eyes. Remember to work in the direction the hair appears to grow.

6 Hook the outline of the head between the ears. Continue this line down along the inner side of the ear and across the base of the ear to the outer edge of each ear. The line will then continue and form the outline of the head on each side of the face. It can end at the chin, or under the chin so check the visual for proper placement, and then hook the rest of this line around the head.

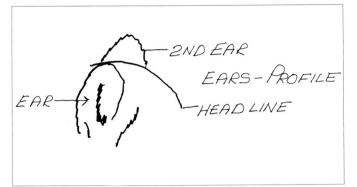

*Bear ear profile*

*Bear ear*

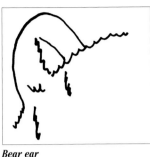

*Bear ear*

7 Start from the completed section between the eyes and hook upward to form the forehead. Before beginning, check to see if this area is divided into layers or sections by lines or shadows. If it's one area, hook up to the outline of the head. If it is several sections, mark the pattern according to what is seen on the visual. Hook the remainder of the forehead over to the outer edge of the head above each eye. When hooking this section be careful to duplicate the curved appearance of the hair as it progresses across the head.

8 Hook the mouth line as it appears. This line continues on to form the outline of the upper jaw and muzzle. Finish the continuation of this line. If the mouth is open hook any teeth or gums that are visible and then the tongue (See section on Teeth and Tongues, page 21.)

9 Hook the area directly below the nose to the mouth line.

10 The muzzle area should be finished next. The outer edge of this area begins at the tip of the upper jaw line and angles up to the inner corner of the eye and adjoins the bridge of the nose. Complete any visible lines, highlights or shadows first and then fill with the correct shades and values.

11 Hook the outline of the chin and then the chin duplicating what is seen on the visual.

12 Next is the cheek area. This will adjoin the muzzle and continue outward to the edge of the face. A line may be noticed that defines this section from the remainder of the face. If so, do this line or shadow first and then the cheek area.

13 Now hook any remaining areas on the face or head. Again these may be defined by lines or shadows, and if so, do them first. Fill each section with the correct shades and values until reaching the edge of the head.

14 The ears are last. Hook the outline of the ear and any hair that grows upward from the base of the ear. Now the rim of the ear should be finished using the visual for guidance, then fill whatever remains in the proper shades and values.

## Bear Profile

1 Hook the outline of the head starting between the ears and down to the mouth line, then extend this line to form the mouth line. (If the mouth is open the line will define the lower edge of the nose and muzzle.) Complete the remainder of the outline around the chin and lower jaw even with the back edge of the mouth line.

2 Next hook the eyes and nose. Refer to sections on Eyes and Nose, pages 15–19.

3 Follow the portions of steps 2 through 5 that apply for Bear's Full Face, page 46.

4 Hook the closest ear first then the outline around the ear and any portion of the rim visible. Any hairs at the base of the ear growing upward should be hooked next. Complete the inner portion of the ear adding any lighter sections first then filling with the darker shades. Should a portion of the back of the ear be showing, do the outline of this section if it hasn't already been done. Any visible highlights or shadows should be finished at this stage and filled with the appropriate shades. If the second ear is evident, hook the outline and follow any of the previous instructions that apply.

5 Follow steps 7, 9, and 10; Bear's Full Face, page 47.

6 Follow steps 11 through 13; Bear's Full Face, page 47.

7 If the bear's mouth is open hook any portion of the teeth and gums visible and then the tongue. (Refer to sections on Teeth, Tongue, and Gums, page 21.)

## Coyotes, Fox and Wolves

These three wild creatures share many physical characteristics with their domestic cousin, the dog. Because of these common traits the same guidelines used for the dog can be used for any one of them.

For me, the most difficult part of the process is finding the right shades of color to create that subtle, multi-colored, mottled look that is seen on all three, but particularly on the coyote and wolf. It's at times like these that I fervently wish more textures (checks, herringbones, plaids, and tweeds) would lend themselves to a narrow cut and not fall apart when I try to hook with them! If you are fortunate enough to have some textures that meet that criteria, use them along with spot dyes, solid color, and occasionally a dip dye to achieve the desired effect.

Don't rush decisions regarding color. Try different combinations until you find the ones that duplicate, to your satisfaction, what is seen on the visual.

### Full Face

1 Hook the eyes and nose (Refer to sections on Eyes, pages 15 & 16, and Dog's Nose, page 17.)

2 Follow steps 1 through 5; Dog's Full Face, pages 25 & 26.

3 Complete the outline of the head between the ears. Notice how this line appears to continue down along the inner side of the ear and in front of the ear to the outer edge of the face or head. Hook the continuation of this line in the correct colors.

4 Follow step 7 through 10; Dog's Full Face, page 26. Follow whatever portion of each step that applies to the animal.

WHERE'S DINNER, *22" x 28", #3-cut wool on rug warp. Designed and hooked by Elizabeth Black, Bentonville, Virginia, 1998.*

5 Finish the remainder of the outline around the face.

6 Follow steps 12 and 13; Dog's Full Face, page 26.

7 Follow directions for Dog's Erect Ears, page 27, and Dog's Full Face, page 27.

All three of these animals have erect ears similar to those on some dogs. If in the process of hooking the ears you discover the animal has hair adjoining both sides of the inner edge of the rim, add what is needed to duplicate the image seen on the visual.

8 After completing the ears, the majority of the face and head will be hooked. However, there may be another section beyond the eye, out to the edge of the head and downward, which isn't hooked. Should this be the case, hook in any directional lines, then highlights and shadows and fill the remaining area with correct colors and values. (Remember to work in the direction the hair grows.)

9 There could be another layer of fur adjoining what was just completed. If so, it will continue down to and possibly under the chin. Hook this the same way the section in step 8 was hooked.

### Profile

1 Hook the eyes and nose. Refer to section on Eyes, pages 15 & 16, and Dog's Nose, page 17.

2 Hook the outline of the face and head starting between the ears and continuing around the face to the neck.

3 Follow Step 1; Dog's Full Face, page 25.

4 Follow steps 3 and 4; Dog's Profile, page 29, to hook the area above and behind the eye and area below the eye.

5 Follow step 4; Dog's Full Face, page 26. (Note: on your animal this may appear as one color.)

6 Follow steps 8 and 9; Dog's Profile, page 29.

*Close up from* INSIDE THE ARK

7 Now hook the outline of the closest ear and any visible rim. Complete any line of color seen at the base of the ear, any hairs growing upwards from the base of the ear, and any hairs growing from the edge of the rim inside the ear. Hook the remainder of the inner ear. (This may consist of one color or several. Duplicate what is seen on the visual.) Make sure there is enough contrast between the various sections of the ear so it doesn't all blend together.

8 Complete the mouth line.

9 If the mouth is open refer to section on Gums, Teeth, and Tongues, page 21.

10 Hook the muzzle. This section, starting at the outline of the face, usually includes a portion above the nose up to the finished section under the eye, continuing down to and including the mouth line, jaw, and jowl.

Refer to step 12; Dog's Full Face, page 26, for guidance in hooking this area.

11 Follow step 9; Coyotes, Fox, and Wolves' Full Face, page 48, if needed.

## Donkey, Mule, Pony and Zebra Faces

S ince the basic structure of this group is so similar to the horse, follow the directions given for the horse's face to hook any of them.

## Additional Information for Zebras

D raw the outlines of any stripes that appear on the face, ears, mane, and neck of the design. Take care in drawing the stripes so they duplicate the same placement seen on the visual. (They help to define the various areas of the face and head.) Hook the black

stripes before hooking the area around them.

When I hook a zebra, I always include a spot dye that is white and spotted with a very, very pale gray. I use a row and sometimes an additional partial row of this spot dye along each side of the black stripes. This imitates that shadow or smudge of color seen between black and white or brown and white (For brown and white use a spot dye of very pale beige and white.) This same spot dye can be used for shadows on other white areas of the zebra. If needed do a second spot dye with the grays a little darker than the first one to use for darker shadows.

RUBY PEARL, *16" x 16", #3- through 8-cut wool on linen. Designed and hooked by Gail Dufresne, Lambertville, New Jersey, 2002.*

## Horned Animals (Goats and Sheep)

I gave directions for hooking cattle with the domestic animals. This section will deal specifically with sheep and goats, but the same steps can be followed to hook any animal face with horns.

## Goats: Domestic and Wild, Full Face

1 Hook the eyes referring to the section on Eyes, pages 15 & 16.

2 Next finish the nose. The shape, size and placement of the nostrils can vary from one species to another. First hook the outline of the nose, then the nostrils. With domestic goats the nostrils may appear to be elongated and tucked up under the upper portion of the nose. On mountain goats the nostrils can be larger and shaped differently.

Duplicate what is seen on the visual. Complete any highlights, shadows or spots of color seen on the nose. Fill the remaining portion of the nose in the proper shades.

3 Hook the mouth line. If the mouth is open, do any visible teeth and gums. Continue by hooking the tongue. (See section on Teeth, Gums, and Tongues, page 21.)

4 Next hook any line extending downward from the center of the base of the nose and intersecting the center of the mouth line.

5 Complete the remainder of the muzzle, the area that surrounds the nose down to the mouth line. Look closely at the visual and a definite outline marking this area will be noticed. (It can also be defined by being a different color or shade than the cheek area.) Finish any highlights and shad-

ows first then fill what remains.

6 Hook the chin area and any highlights and shadows seen, then fill what remains.

7 Refer to steps 3 through 7; Bear's Full Face, pages 46 & 47.

8 Refer to steps 12 and 13; Bear's Full Face, page 47.

9 The horns appear to grow right behind the line defining the forehead from the remainder of the head, including the ears. Hook the outlines of the horns just as they appear on the visual and any definition lines on the horns. (You don't have to include every line, just enough to give the suggestion of what's really there.) Complete any highlights or shadows and fill whatever remains in the proper shades.

10 Finish any remaining portion of the head visible behind the horns.

*Mountain goat ear*

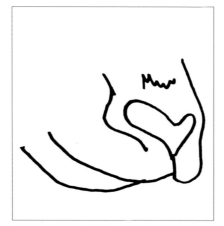

*Mountain goat profile*

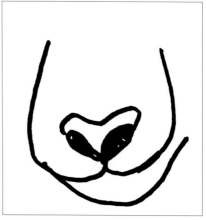

*Wild sheep frontal*

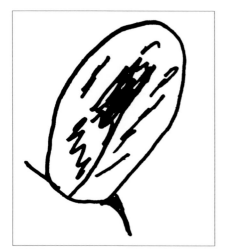

*Wild sheep ear*

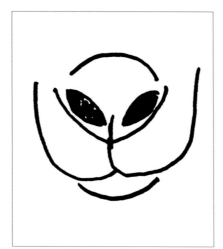

*Mountain goat nose*

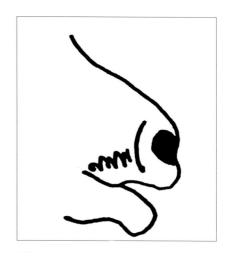

*Wild sheep profile*

## Ears

ERECT EARS: Hook the outline of the ear and any rim visible inside the ear attached to the rim. Complete any highlights or shadows visible inside the ear, then whatever inside portion of the ear remains. Work any outer section of the ear. If only the back of the ear is seen, hook the outline of any visible rim, any highlights or shadows, and fill what remains. LOP EARS: Finish the outline of the outside portion of the ear first, adding any visible rim. Next complete any spots or patterns of color seen on the ear. Add any highlights and shadows and fill what remains. If a portion of the inner ear is evident hook the outline,

highlights, and shadows and fill what remains.

## Profile

1 Refer to steps 1 and 2; Antlered Animal's Profile, page 43.

2 Refer to steps 2 and 3; Horse's Profile, page 31.

3 Hook the nose and mouth line. Refer to steps 2 and 3; Horned Animals' Full Face, page 50.

4 Complete the muzzle area. Refer to steps 4 and 5; Horned Animals' Full Face, page 50.

5 Finish the chin area. The chin is the area below the mouth line that continues back to approximately the outer

edge of the mouth line. Any spots of color should be hooked first, then add any highlights and shadows, and fill what remains. Be careful to work in the direction the hair grows. If the goat has chin whiskers, do them now. Start by hooking any obvious lines that separate colors or act as directional lines. Continue by adding highlights and shadows and fill what remains.

6 Hook the closest ear. Refer to step 1; Goat's Full Face, page 50. Follow the instructions that describe the goat's ear.

7 Complete the center section of the face up to the top of the forehead. This includes any area above the nose

and along the inside of the eye and out to the outline of the head. It also includes the area directly below the nose and above the mouth line that hasn't been finished.

Hook any spots, stripes, or definition lines, then the highlights and shadows, and fill what remains. Work in the direction the hair appears to grow.

**8** Complete the cheek area and any remaining portions above and below the eye.

**9** Hook the horns. Follow steps 9 and 10; Horned Animals' Full Face, page 50.

**10** Complete any unfinished area of the head.

**11** Hooking the neck is started with doing the outline. Any definition lines or spots of color should be hooked next, then the highlights and shadows, and fill what remains. Remember to work in the direction the hair follows.

## Sheep: Domestic and Wild, Full Face

**1** Hook the eyes referring to the section on Eyes, pages 15 & 16.

**2** Hook the outline of the nose and the nostrils. (Try to duplicate the shape seen on the visual.) Hook any highlights, shadows or spots of color in the area surrounding the nostrils and fill any remaining area with the proper shades of color.

**3** Refer to steps 3 and 4; Horned Animals, Goats Full Face, page 50.

**4** Refer to steps 5 and 6; Horned Animals, Goats Full Face, page 50.

**5** Refer to steps 3 through 6; Bears' Full Face, page 46.

**6** Start from the completed section between the eyes and hook upward, to form the forehead. (However if the sheep has long hair covering the fore-

*LYDIA, 33" x 45", #6-cut wool on burlap. Designed and hooked by Patty Yoder, Tinmouth, Vermont, 1993.*

head, do it before this section above the eyes is hooked.) If the forehead area appears to be more than one section, mark the sections on the pattern and hook them as they appear on the visual. Now finish the remainder of the forehead, above the eyes to the outer edge of the head. (Duplicate the direction the hair follows.)

**7** If the sheep doesn't have horns, hook the ears now. Refer to step 11; Horned Animals, Goats' Profile, page 50. Complete any unfinished areas on the head.

*COCO, 14 1/2" x 22 1/2", #3-cut wool on wool backing. Designed and hooked by Liz Marino, South Egremont, Massachusetts, 2000.*

**8** To hook the neck read the sections for hooking the body of the animal that apply. **HORNED SHEEP:** If both horns and ears are present study the visual to determine whether the horns lie over the ears or vice versa. Hook whatever is the top layer or what is closest first. (Example; if the ear lies over the horn, hook the ear first.)

**9** Refer to steps 9 and 11; Horned Animals, Goat's Profile, page 50.

**10** Complete any remaining portion of the head visible behind the ears and horns.

## Sheep in Profile

**1** Refer to steps 1 and 2; Antlered Animals Profile, page 43.

**2** Hook the outline of the nose then the nostrils duplicating the shape seen on the visual. Next finish any highlights, shadows, or spots of color surrounding the nostrils. Fill any remaining area with the proper shades of color.

**3** Refer to steps 3 and 4; Horned Animals, Goat's Full Face, page 50.

**4** Refer to steps 5 through 10; Goats' Profile, pages 51 & 52, to complete your sheep in profile.

# CHAPTER 10

# THE BODY

PEACEABLE KINGDOM, 49" x 35", #3-cut wool on rug warp. Designed and hooked by Elizabeth Black, Bentonville, Virginia, 1997.

DALMATION PILLOW, 18" x 18", #3-cut wool on rug warp. Designed and hooked by Elizabeth Black, Bentonville, Virginia, 1998.

I cannot emphasize enough how important it is to have the animal's body well drawn. It is an integral part of a successful project. The bone and muscle structure become your guides in determining the placement of color to form highlights, shadows, and contours in both long and shorthaired animals.

I approach hooking the body of an animal just as I do a face; as a series of layers and sections. All animals break down into three basic sections: the forequarters, midsection, and hindquarters. This division is more visible on shorthaired animals, but is found on both.

## Shorthaired and Longhaired Animals in Profile

In profile the forequarters and hindquarters are "top layers" as they lie over the midsection and should be hooked before the midsection. Think of the forequarters as the shoulder and leg area that lie over the neck and chest area. There are two options with a short haired animal; hook

a holding line on the portion of the forequarter that adjoins the neck and chest and complete the neck and chest first, or hook the forequarter first and then the neck and chest.

On the longhaired animal, the hair on the neck may be layered and partially cover the throat and overlap the front line of the forequarter. If this is the case hook the neck first and then the throat and forequarter.

If the upper outline of the animal is multicolored, hook it as you do each sec-

tion. Should the line basically be one color, hook the entire line before finishing any of the sections. Complete the bottom line on the midsection in the same manner.

The hindquarters consist of the hips, rear legs, and buttock area. The midsection is what remains between the two other sections.

## Shorthaired Animals - General Directions

Complete any definition lines between the two sections and any additional definition lines within the sec-

LITTLE PRINCESS, 22" x 14", #3-cut wool on rug warp. Designed by Elizabeth Black. Hooked by Barbara Calvo, Whitehouse Station, New Jersey, 2003.

tion about to be hooked. Determine the direction the hair grows in this section. (It can go in more than one direction. Draw a few guidelines with a marker to duplicate the direction the hair follows.) Any highlights or shadows in the section being worked should now be included, then fill whatever remains. (Remember to hook in the direction the hair grows.) Repeat the process in each section. When all three sections have been completed, hook any part of the body and the remaining legs that are visible. Follow the same procedure used in hooking the various sections to finish the legs.

## Longhaired Animals - General Directions

The major differences in hooking long-haired animals is that the structure of the animal isn't as pronounced and the fur is a series of layers. Follow the general directions given for the shorthaired animal plus the following: Notice how each section of the body can consist of multiple layers of hair that can grow in different directions. As each section is completed, hook what appears as the top layer first and work your way down through each layer. Remember the bottom edge of each layer may be uneven to reflect the variation in the length of the fur. Use the visual for guidance.

## Shorthaired and Longhaired Animals - Laying down

Follow the same steps used to hook the animal in profile and any of the following steps that apply. Depending on the position of the animal, the back leg may lie over a portion of the midsection. If this is the case, hook the leg and paw first. Sometimes the tail wraps

MAC AND RUFOUS, *39" x 29", #3- and 5-cut on rug warp. Designed by Elizabeth Black. Hooked by Barbara Beck-Wilczek, Littleton, New Hampshire, 2003.*

around and covers a portion of the back leg, paw, and midsection. In this case do the tail first, then the leg, the paw, and the midsection last.

## Shorthaired Standing and Sitting - Frontal View

In this position, the forequarters of the animal are mainly seen; neck, shoulders, chest, belly, and front legs. Hook any outline of the neck, shoulders, and chest as it appears on the visual.

Starting with the neck and shoulder area hook in any definition lines that signify the muscle structure or the throat area. There may also be lines that create folds or wrinkles or stripes. Complete any of the lines that are present. If spots or lines that divide changes of color are visible, hook these lines. When you finish these various lines be careful to duplicate the direction they follow and use the correct shades of color. Add any highlights or shadows in the correct shades and fill what remains.

Continue the outline of the body along the outer edge of the animal and around the legs and paws.

Hook the chest area following the same procedure used for the neck and shoulder area. First complete the legs and paws (Refer to the section on Paws, page 55.), and then hook the belly area. Follow the same procedures as you did for the rest of the body. Next finish any other sections of the body that are partially visible.

## Longhaired Standing and Sitting Frontal View

In addition to following the basic instructions given for the frontal views of the shorthaired animal that apply; remember in this case the hair will appear to be layered.

Hook the top layer directly under the chin first and any highlights or shadows first. Fill what remains using the proper shades and values. Continue to the next layer under the one just completed. Work each layer in the same manner until the chest and belly areas are completed. Remember to work in the direction the hair appears to follow. Next do the legs and paws (Refer to section on Paws, page 55.) If the fur appears to be layered on the legs, fol-

*Close up from* **WAITING FOR THE VET**

low the same procedure used in hooking the chest and belly. Finish any remaining sections of the body that are partially visible.

## Front View Lying Down; Short and Longhaired Animals

Follow the same basic instructions given for the sitting or standing positions. Should one or both front legs lie across the chest, do them first, then the chest. If additional sections of the body are visible, finish them after the chest and forequarters have been hooked.

## Stripes, Spots, and Patterns

Notice how the stripes on a tiger or zebra change direction on various portions of their bodies and how the stripes help define the three basic sections of each body. The stripe may also serve as the definition line between two sections or another line may divide the sections. Hook whichever applies to the animal. If it's a line it can be a highlight or a shadow so refer to the visual for guidance. First complete the stripes in the section you are working and then any highlights and shadows that are present; fill what remains.

Some animals, such as the clouded leopard and the reticulated giraffe, have a coat pattern of even-edged markings that appear to be separated by a network of color. Hook any definition lines that appear between the sections. Next complete the "network" in the section you've chosen and then the markings. Add any highlights and shadows and fill what remains.

## Hooves, Paws and Tails

**HOOVES:** I try to keep these as simple as possible. The horse's hoof is one solid area while other animals such as pigs, cows, and deer have cloven hooves. In either case do the outline of the hoof first and if it is cloven, hook the division line on the hoof if visible. Hook any shadows or highlights present and fill what remains.

**PAWS:** Outline the paw in the correct shades and values. Hook the division lines between the toes. If the division lines between the toes appear to connect in a slightly curved line across the top of the toes, hook this continuation of the division lines now. Next hook any portion of the claws to be included. I find them to be distracting and rather ugly so I keep them as small and unobtrusive as possible. Many times, on cats and dogs, I eliminate them entirely. If a portion of the pads

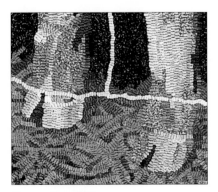

*Close up from* **LYDIA**

are visible on the foot do them now. Don't make them too large. Hook any highlights or shadows that appear on the toes. (This is the area below the curved line that was formed by the continuation of the lines between the toes.) Fill any area on the toes that remains. Any definition lines, highlights, shadows, or wrinkles that are visible above the completed "toe" area should be finished now and fill whatever remains.

If a large portion of the paw is covered with hair, hook the hair that lies over the paw first and then the remainder of the paw following the above-mentioned steps.

**SHORTHAIRED TAILS:** Hook the outline of the tail. Study the visual to see if there are any definition lines on the tail and if so, hook these lines duplicating the direction they follow, then complete any highlights and shadows that are visible and fill what remains.

**LONGHAIRED TAILS:** Some tails, such as a horse's, may appear to be all one length. In this case hook the outline of the tail and any definition lines seen on the tail first, then any highlights or shadows that are visible. On some animals the tail may consist of a series of layers of hair. First hook the outline of the tail. Start with the top layer hooking in any highlights or shadows. Fill in the remainder of the layer being careful to work in the direction the hair follows. Continue to do each layer in the same manner until the tail is completed.

On other animals the hair grows outward from a natural part or line that occurs in the center portion of the tail. This center portion is often darker than the rest of the tail. Hook outward from this center area in the direction the hair follows. Use the visual as a guide.

# CHAPTER 11

# HOOKING BACKGROUNDS

**FOX RUG,** *7' x 5', #3-cut wool on rug warp. Designed and hooked by Elizabeth Black, Bentonville, Virginia, 1992.*

## Backgrounds

For years the overwhelming consensus has been that the background color must be chosen first and then the remainder of the project can be color planned. As my level of expertise grew and my designs became more complex, I found myself becoming more and more frustrated with this rule. I learned from experience that spending hours doing a color rendering of my design was a waste of time for me. Why? Because until I actually hooked some of the colors I had chosen into my piece, I didn't know if they would work the way I intended. If I wasn't satis-

fied with the effect, I would continue to change the colors until achieving the look I wanted. Sometimes this resulted in major changes from what I had originally planned. So what's the problem? The changes I'd made no longer worked with the background color. After sacrificing color choices several times to accommodate the background color, I decided I was going to ignore "the rule." First I hook my design, and then I choose a back-

**UNTITLED TIGER PILLOW,** *19 1/2" diameter, #3- and 4-cut wool on rug warp. Designed and hooked by Roberta Smith, West Windsor, New Jersey, 2003.*

911, 52" x 36", #3-cut wool on rug warp. Designed and hooked by Elizabeth Black, Bentonville, Virginia, 1996.

TIGERS IN PARADISE, 5' x 3 ¹/₂', #3, 4, and 5-cut wool on rug warp. Designed by Elizabeth Black. Hooked by Theresa Strack, Benford, New Hampshire, 2003.

ground color. Working in this manner has given me the freedom to change my mind and experiment with various color combinations. Contrary to what many people think, it's not that difficult to find a suitable background shade after the rest of the piece is completed.

If I am working on a commission rug, the client may specify that a certain color be used in the background. In this case I must plan the rest of my color pallet around their choice.

I prefer to keep the backgrounds very simple in most of my rugs. However, occasionally I combine several spot dyes in very subtle shades of one color to create some movement and color variations in the background. The key to doing this successfully is by making sure the color change is so subtle that it all blends and gives the effect of a moiré or water silk fabric. Should the background be distracting the eye from the design, then it is not subtle enough.

I am not a fan of incorporating squiggles or other patterns into backgrounds, as I find them very distracting. Remember, if the eye goes immediately to the background and then to the design, perhaps the background is too much of a focal point.

When I do the background I prefer to hook around the design shapes so it doesn't look like straight lines of background color. If I reach a point where my hooking is becoming a straight line, I add several short partial rows, each shorter than the other, directly below what has become a straight line. When I hook the next full row I will have to curve around the added partial rows and this will put a curve back into my hooking.

## Pictorials

When hooking a pictorial, I think of the pattern as two basic components; design and background. I define design as all of the elements that are focal points in the piece. The background is viewed as the portions surrounding and supporting the major design elements.

My pictorial, *Pigtorial* (based on a photo taken by Robert Dowling who gave me written permission to use it as my visual in creating this piece) breaks down into three distinct areas. The pigs are the focal point. The straw is very apparent but secondary to the pigs, and it functions as a base for the piece. By using primarily black for the remaining area a sharp contrast was created between the animals, the straw, and the wall. This sharp contrast is what gives dimension to the piece.

In *Waiting for the Vet*, the important design elements are the animals, the flowers areas secondary, and all the rest of the areas as support or background for the focal point—the animals.

Barbara Lextrom wanted a sharp contrast between her polar bears and sky. Hooking the skyline and northern lights

PIGTORIAL, *40" x 30", #3-cut wool on rug warp. Designed and hooked by Elizabeth Black, Bentonville, Virginia, 1999.*

BIJOU, *26" x 36", #3 and 4-cut wool on monk's cloth, Pattern from Hues and Views Images, Inc. Hooked by Susan Naples, Santa Ana, California, 2003.*

with several dip dyes in dark and medium shades created the effect she desired and added interest to the piece without overwhelming the bears.

If you're hooking a smaller piece to use as a pillow or picture, keep the following in mind: Choose a color that will create a definite contrast between the design and background and keep the background subtle so it doesn't detract from the design.

This doesn't mean you can't use a texture, spot dye, or dip dye; just don't let it take over the piece. Remember, if the eye goes directly to the background and then to the design, perhaps it's time to rethink the background, as it has become the dominant factor.

Notice how in Carol Murphy's rug of the horse, *Jazz,* the background color is a pleasing contrast to the horse and enhances the piece without diverting attention from the focal point.

## Dummy Boards

**FINISHING A DUMMY BOARD:** Over the years I have designed and hooked numerous dummy boards or as they were originally called "lonesome companions."

After completing the hooking, my late husband took over and finished them for me. He said I was too impatient with this part of the project and would end up doing a mediocre job! The following instructions outline his method for mounting the work.

**SUPPLIES NEEDED:**

- Elmer's™ white glue
- Plywood: $1/2$" thick for small and medium boards, $3/4$" for tall or large board. (The additional thickness helps prevent warping.)
- Staples and a staple gun; $1/4$" and $5/16$" staples.
- **FABRIC: OPTION 1** Black felt, flannel, or

**ABOVE:** *JAZZ, 22" x 23", #3-cut wool on rug warp. Designed and hooked by Carol Murphy, Hopkinton, New Hampshire, 1995.* **BELOW:** WAITING FOR THE VET, *45" x 32", #3-cut wool on rug warp. Designed and hooked by Elizabeth Black, Bentonville, Virginia, 1994.*

POLAR BEARS DUMMY BOARD, *38" x 32", #3-cut wool on rug warp. Designed by Elizabeth Black. Hooked by Barbara Lextrom, Annandale, Virginia, 2003.*

other tightly woven fabric. I choose black because it doesn't detract from the hooking. OPTION 2 Use several tightly woven fabrics that repeat the colors

seen on the outer edges of the hooked piece. This takes additional time and work but is well worth the effort.

OPTION 3 Instead of using regular fabric,

substitute suede cloth, suede or leather in shades that match the colors seen on the outer edges of the hooking. (If using leather, use the wrong side, as it looks more like fur or hair.) Many fabric shops have reasonably priced remnants of these items. This became my husband's favorite way to finish the boards even though it entailed more time and effort.

■ Wood: A piece to fashion a wood stand.
■ Stain or Paint: For the wood stand.
■ Hinges: Two

The best way to proceed is to enlist the help of a person who is familiar with using the tools needed for this project! However, if this isn't possible you can successfully complete this project on your own. I suggest that you, or the person helping, read and reread the instructions that follow so they will be thoroughly understood before proceeding.

After the piece is hooked, glue completely all around the hooked area (glue

WELSH CORGI, *15" x 15", #3-cut wool on burlap. Designed and hooked by Margaret Brightbill, Titusville, New Jersey, 1999.*

KITTEN DUMMY BOARD, *11" x 15", #3-cut wool on rug warp. Designed and hooked by Elizabeth Black, Bentonville, Virginia, 1990;* GIRL WITH CHICKEN, *20" x 41", #3-cut wool on rug warp. Designed and hooked by Elizabeth Black, Bentonville, Virginia, 1990;* COLLIE DUMMY BOARD, *18" x 24", #3-cut wool on rug warp. Designed and hooked by Elizabeth Black, Bentonville, Virginia, 1991.*

as close to the hooking as possible without getting glue on the wool.) Use a small plastic scraper (an old credit card works well) and work away from the hooking to

PUG DUMMY BOARD, *20" x 35", #3 and 4-cut wool on rug warp. Designed and hooked by Elizabeth Black, Bentonville, Virginia, 1990.*

spread the glue about 2" wide around the entire design. After the glue is dry, stretch the glued area.

Lay the hooked pattern on the piece of plywood (waterproof is best). Stretch the pattern and staple it with $^1/4$" Arrow T-50 staples, all around the edge of the backing fabric.

Using a punch, pick, or hardwood nail, make a pattern on the plywood by following the outer edge of the design. The marks made in the plywood by doing this should be approximately $^1/2$" apart. Remove the hooked piece from the plywood and connect the indentations so that there is a solid indented line that matches the outline of the piece. Cut the plywood pattern out on the line then cut hooked pattern at the outer glued edge. Turn the hooked pattern face down and lay plywood pattern on hooked piece. Pull edges of hooked

piece over the back of the plywood and staple (with $^5/16$" staples securely over the plywood all the way around).

## Finishing the Piece

To cover the outer edge of the design cut enough strips of fabric 12" long and 3" wide to go around the entire board. If you are using option 2 or 3 cut your strips 3" wide and the appropriate length to match the color of the hooking.

On the front side of the board, lay a cut strip of fabric as close to the hooking as possible. This should be positioned so the 3" width of the fabric is toward the center of the board.

Staple with $^5/16$" staples at a 45-degree angle (or glue) as close to the hooking as possible, all around the board.

Turn over just glued or stapled fabric to backside of plywood. Cut one piece of

**GUS DUMMY BOARD**, *23" x 19", #3-cut wool on rug warp. Designed and hooked by Elizabeth Black, Bentonville, Virginia, 1993.*

fabric to cover the back of the board. Cut it approximately ¹/₂" larger than the board all along its perimeters. Staple or glue it to the back, folding edges under as you go. This will finish the back of the board and help to protect the work. If using staples, a nice finishing touch is to position a brass upholsterer's tack over each staple.

Cut a piece of board or plywood for the stand (this has the effect of a rudder) and attach it to the dummy board with two hinges.

Now stand your work in a conspicuous place and enjoy the compliments you will receive!

## Inspiration for Design

Since first discovering rug hooking, my head has been filled with an endless variety of ideas to turn into designs. The possibilities for design are everywhere just waiting to be adapted into another project.

Having said that, I realize creating an original work may not be that easy for everyone. But there are simple things you

can begin to do that will help get the creative juices flowing.

First of all, rid yourself of that mental block that keeps you from trying to create an original work. I firmly believe everyone has more creative ability than they think they have. If you keep telling yourself "Oh I can't do that" it will become a self-fulfilling prophecy.

Over the years many of my designs have been inspired by memories of incidents that have occurred in my life. Other ideas just seem to appear out of thin air. I believe these are really partially developed thoughts that have been tucked away in my subconscious just waiting for the right moment to reveal themselves.

Regardless of the source I welcome these seeds of inspiration. However, I know if I don't write them down within a few hours time I will be racking my brain trying to remember the great idea I had! Because of my moments of "lack of recall" I began to keep a notebook of ideas and thoughts that could later be used to develop various projects. Sometimes it's just a

few words or a sentence to jog my memory. Other times I may write a paragraph describing particular elements I want to consider using in a piece. Certain ideas don't always generate the same amount of enthusiasm as they did when I first wrote them down, but sometime in the future my interest may return, and I haven't lost that original idea.

I guess one could call the list my "confidence blanket," as I know with it in hand I'll never have to stare at a blank piece of backing and wonder what to put on it.

A good example of how well my list has served me is one of my latest rugs. First you must understand that every stray cat in the county seems to know I'm a soft touch for food and outdoor accommodations until something better becomes available. Of course, if you are feeding domestic strays, the lunch counter is often visited by other free loaders; such as raccoons and possums.

I live in an old house with a wrap-around porch and would occasionally feed my motley crew on the portion of the porch near the kitchen door. One evening I looked out to see who was dining and was confronted with quite a sight. There sat a mother cat with her brood staring at a tiny possum that was gobbling up their dinner! The attitudes and looks ran the gambit from curiosity to disbelief, fear, and last but not least, indignation. After several moments one kitten gathered up the courage and with a great deal of bravado arched his back, did his best to look intimidating, and swatted the possum's tail. The next thing I knew, food was flying through the air while the terrified little possum ran in one direction and the cats in another. Such drama!

I was still chuckling over the events that had just unfolded as I made another

CATS, 17" x 60", #3-cut wool on rug warp. Designed by Elizabeth Black. Hooked by Sibyl Osicka, Parma, Ohio, 1997.

UNINVITED GUEST, 48" x 36", #3-cut wool on rug warp. Designed and hooked by Elizabeth Black, Bentonville, Virginia, 2003.

entry in my ideas and inspiration notebook. This entry was the basis for the rug entitled *The Uninvited Guest*. Such every day happenings, not all so dramatic, have served as the inspiration for some of my pieces. All of the photos of work shown in this chapter, some mine and some by my students have been inspired or partially inspired by animals.

Theresa Strack combined photos of scenery she had taken on one vacation with some of the tigers she had viewed in Sigfreid and Roy's performance in Las Vegas. Barbara Personette used a photo she took of her dog, Maxine, pursuing one of her favorite pastimes; guarding her dish. A poem was Ann Winterling's inspiration for her tiger dummyboard and Gene Shepherd used segments of a famous poem mentioning cats and fog and combined it with his house and neighbors' homes to create an unusual pictorial. Liz Marino chose to immortalize one of her llamas on a wall hanging and Sibyl Osicka captured a true likeness of her wonderful Persian cats in another wall hanging.

These examples give an indication how simple ideas and everyday events can be transformed into wonderful pieces.

Still having doubts about coming up with a worthy idea? Then, start out by taking a stamped pattern you've purchased and enhance it with your own ideas. The lines on a pattern are only guidelines, and as far as I know, the pattern doesn't come with a warning suggesting severe penalties if it is tampered with!

Another wonderful source for inspiration is a child's or grandchild's drawing or painting. Take the original and enlarge it to the desired size, transfer onto backing, and hook a lasting family memory (Be sure to use the same colors as seen on the original as this is part of the charm.) This is also a good project for a child wanting to learn how to hook. This same concept can be applied and used with any family photo you wish to copy to create a permanent remembrance of a special person, time, or place. Many times I find a simple occurrence or memory can be the inspi-

**FOG,** 69 ½" x 33", #3- and 5-cut wool on cotton rug warp. Designed and hooked by Gene Shepherd, Anaheim, California, 2001.

ration for a good piece. If something catches your interest or attention add it to the list of ideas for future use.

When you come upon a beautiful piece of wool that draws you like a moth to a flame, buy it! Any time you are that attracted to a piece of wool, I guarantee you will not only use it but it may serve as the catalyst for a new design. Feeling guilty about adding more wool to your inventory? Don't. The more wool, the better the choice and the more opportunity to expand your use of color and create a wonderful piece. I refuse to believe that I can have too much wool!

For a number of years the majority of my work has revolved around commissioned pieces and this has been both challenging and rewarding. Some commissions are very straight forward; such as a realistic likeness of a certain animal or beloved pet. Once I have several good photos of my subject it is not too difficult to create a piece that will satisfy my client.

Other times I'll receive a request to incorporate a portion of the color and design found in drapes or upholstery. This simplifies my task, as I already have a color palette established as well as some direction for design.

However, a large percentage of people are uncertain as to what they want or really like, so then it's up to me to come up with a design that pleases them and is appropriate for the room. I have discovered one of the best ways to do this is to ask them what they don't like or want. Once I have eliminated all of their "don't wants" I'm left with a short list of possible color and design choices.

Sometimes an individual approaches me with an idea that they are much more enthused about than I am. When asked to create a wall hanging depicting Noah's ark, my initial reaction was, it's been done, redone, and overdone; how can I approach it in a different manner? After mulling the idea over for several weeks and looking at various interpretations of the ark, it dawned on me. Practically

everything I saw dealt with the exterior of the ark. Why not do a wallhanging depicting the animals inside the ark? The time I spent studying how the ark has been interpreted in other works helped me discover a different approach to my project. Once I had the unique idea in hand I had more than enough inspiration to create *Inside the Ark*.

Inspiration for design can be found in all areas of our lives: family, pets, friends, nature books, poetry, joy, and even tragedy. Hooking with friends, attending workshops, rug camps, teaching, and rug exhibits can boost your enthusiasm and inspire your work. Just open your eyes and your mind and the ideas will come!

A footnote to my possum and cat saga—the little possum's hunger pangs outweighed his fear and he came at least once a day to eat. Within a few days he and the kittens were gathering around the dish together and sharing their meals. I just love a happy ending!